Becoming a College Writer

A Student Workbook

Edition 1.0

Adam Karnes & Laura Scott

Becoming a College Writer: A Student Workbook

© 2022 Chemeketa Community College

ISBN-13: 978-1-955499-13-2

Chemeketa Press
Chemeketa Community College
4000 Lancaster Dr NE
Salem, Oregon 97305
collegepress@chemeketa.edu
chemeketapress.org

For desk copies or ordering inquiries, contact collegepress@chemeketa.edu.

Cover design by Abbey Gaterud
Cover photo by Hans-Peter Gauster on Unsplash
Interior design by Ronald Cox IV, Abbey Gaterud
Student sample essay by Kevin Anderson

Land Acknowledgment

Chemeketa Press is located on the land of the Kalapuya, who today are represented by the Confederated Tribes of the Grand Ronde and the Confederated Tribes of the Siletz Indians, whose relationship with this land continues to this day. We offer gratitude for the land itself, for those who have stewarded it for generations, and for the opportunity to study, learn, work, and be in community on this land. We acknowledge that our College's history, like many others, is fundamentally tied to the first colonial developments in the Willamette Valley in Oregon. Finally, we respectfully acknowledge and honor past, present, and future Indigenous students of Chemeketa Community College.

Contents

Part 1

Writing Process

Many students approach their writing without a process. A **process** is a specific approach for completing an often-repeated task. For example, some people always follow a specific series of actions when they leave their house—they grab their keys, put their phone in a pocket, turn off the lights, and lock the door. That's a simple process, but following it makes the act of leaving the house quick and complete.

While it's possible to write without a process, you'll have better results if you make a plan. Instead of waiting until the hour before an assignment is due and completing an essay in one session, begin your writing early and complete your tasks in several steps.

This section describes one approach to the writing process. You may have tried a different way in the past, perhaps with a different number of steps or different names. The most important thing is to find a method that works for your writing. Doing so will cause less stress and likely give you better results.

This book recommends the following steps:

1. Prewriting
2. Planning
3. Drafting
4. Revising
5. Editing

1. Prewriting

Before you begin writing at length, take some time to explore your ideas. When students stare at a blank page and call it writer's block, it's often a because they didn't work through the possible topics and approaches to their writing assignments before drafting.

Prewriting involves answering basic questions that will guide your drafting. Those questions might include, "What is my topic?" or "How large is my topic?" You can answer these questions to prepare for drafting. You've probably done prewriting exercises already. Some of the most common exercises are brainstorming, mind-mapping, freewriting, and looping.

A. Use Brainstorming

Brainstorming is the act of listing potential topics. These ideas could be the main topic for an entire essay, but they could also be the subtopics and details that support your main topic.

When you brainstorm, be kind to yourself. Try not to judge your ideas. Focus on making a long list, not on making a perfect one (figure 1.1.1). You can always skip any topics you don't like when you're done. Push yourself to think of more ideas than the few that immediately come to mind. This will increase your productivity.

Try This

1. Set a timer for 5–10 minutes.
2. List topics in no particular order.
3. Put your ideas on the page without judgment.
4. If you feel like stopping before the time is done, keep going anyway.
5. When the timer is done, look at your list. Ask the following questions:
    a. Which topics could be the basis for your thesis?
    b. Which topics could be a subtopic, supporting idea, or example?
    c. Which topics are too small or not related to the assignment?
4. If one of the topics seems promising, do another brainstorm with this topic as a starting point.

Figure 1.1.1. Brainstorming Sample. This list shows a brainstorming exercise for an assignment about a personal experience that changed someone's view about something.

Travel

Studying abroad   Visiting Europe

   My host family   Different buildings

   New friends

Language barrier

   Trying to order food

Getting over fears   Strange customs

   Mass transportation   Different food

   Getting lost   24-hour clocks

Memories

   Wanting to go back

B. Use Mind-Mapping

If you like to think in images, mind-mapping can be a helpful exercise. This activity is sometimes called clustering or webbing. **Mind-mapping** is arranging ideas on a page to reflect relationships. It is like brainstorming because you are listing ideas. But the difference lies in how you use the entire page to connect your ideas. You may find that the mind-map helps you to think of more ideas by picturing how similar or different your ideas are to each other (figure 1.1.2).

Try This

1. Begin with a blank piece of paper.
2. Write a topic idea in the center of the paper.
3. Write other topic ideas on the paper, but place each in a location that shows its relationship to the ideas already on the page. Similar ideas should be placed close together. Different ideas should be placed farther apart.
4. As you write ideas, draw lines between related ideas to show connections.
5. When you've filled the page, you should have a map that shows the relationship between topics and subtopics (smaller ideas).
6. Review your mind-map, and consider which ideas could work for your project. Which ideas are too big? Which ideas are too small or not related? Which ideas work with your assignment?
7. You may want to do another mind-map starting with a more specific topic taken from the first mind map.

Figure 1.1.2. Mind-Mapping Sample. This image shows how you can use the page to connect ideas or identify opportunities for new ideas.

Meeting my first
new friend

Dinner time

Feeling isolated

No hats

Nobody like me

Clothes

Different interests

Strange customs

New friends

Studying abroad

Dealing with homesickness

Trying new things

Long phone
calls with
mom

Different food

Social media

Comic books

Missing
my dog

Train travel

Missing
my house

Museums

C. Use Freewriting

Freewriting is when you write without stopping in order to explore one or more potential topics in sentences. The key to a successful freewriting session is to keep writing, even if you feel as if you've run out of good ideas (figure 1.1.3). Don't stop to ask yourself whether your ideas are good. Just keep writing until you're done.

Try This

1. Choose a broad topic or use the topic given by your instructor.
2. Set a target time for your writing. Five minutes is a good amount of time when starting out. Use a timer you cannot see so that you do not lose your focus.
3. On a blank page, write on the topic for the full time. Do not stop writing until the time is up. Keep your fingers typing or your pen moving the entire time. If you can't think of something, write something like, "I can't think of anything," or "This is a freewrite." Eventually, a new idea will come.
4. Be kind to yourself and your ideas. Write whatever you're thinking, even if it's silly, boring, or random.
5. Stop when the time is up. Take a break before doing more writing.

Figure 1.1.3. Freewriting Sample. Freewriting is a strategy to generate a lot of new material and ideas.

A personal experience that changed my mind. I think my study abroad program applies here. What did I learn. Let's see. Thinking thinking thinking. My time with the host family is the strongest memory. I think that they were so kind and so welcoming and they taught me about their culture. They became my friends during a time when I wasn't sure I'd made the right decision. I wondered if I would have been happier staying home that term, but they convinced me that it was the right idea. Also they convinced me that their country and their culture was cool even though I wasn't sure at first. It was mostly my mom's idea that I try going because she did it too, so I was a little bit mad at her, but it ended up being a great idea.

The student is beginning with a topic from an assignment.

It's okay to just write what you're thinking, even if it doesn't make sense.

A freewrite will often change topics unexpectedly. Don't stop to improve it. Just write your thoughts as they occur to you.

D. Use Looping

One of the best ways to prewrite is to combine multiple freewrites through the process of looping. When **looping**, a writer begins with a single freewriting session, followed by some analysis (looking at the parts) and reflection (deep thinking). Then, the writer completes another freewrite, using a specific idea pulled from the first session. Repeat this process as many times as necessary to develop a topic narrow enough to satisfy an assignment (figure 1.1.4a–c).

Try This

1. Complete a freewriting session. Follow the steps described in the section on freewriting.
2. When you're done, read your freewrite and do some reflecting. Which parts are especially interesting? Which parts relate well to the assignment? Look for the section that does the best job of explaining a potential topic. Choose your best section from the freewrite. Draw a circle around this section.
3. Do another freewrite, but this time, begin with the section that you circled from the first freewrite. Use the ideas from this section as your starting point.
4. When you're done with this second freewrite, go through the same process of review and selection.
5. Continue looping as many times as necessary to narrow your topic.

Figure 1.1.4a. Looping Sample, Part 1. This writing strategy combines multiple freewriting sessions paired with analysis and reflection.

A personal experience that changed my mind. I think my study abroad program applies here. What did I learn. Let's see. Thinking thinking thinking. My time with the host family is the strongest memory. I think that they were so kind and so welcoming and they taught me about their culture. They became my friends during a time when I wasn't sure I'd made the right decision. I wondered if I would have been happier staying home that term, but they convinced me that it was the right idea. Also they convinced me that their country and their culture was cool even though I wasn't sure at first. It was mostly my mom's idea that I try going because she did it too, so I was a little bit mad at her, but it ended up being a great idea.

When looping, take one idea from a freewrite and make it the focus of another freewrite. This author chooses the idea of learning about another culture while living in a different country.

Figure 1.1.4b. Looping Sample, Part 2. This writing strategy combines multiple freewriting sessions paired with analysis and reflection.

(Learning about a new culture.) My host family was kind, but they really wouldn't take no for an answer when I was scared to experience new things. I remember that first dinner when they served that weird soup. I was not a fan of the vegetables, but they just sat there waiting for me to try it, and I could tell the sister especially was a little offended. It really wasn't that bad, and it was nice to see how much it made them happy when I tried it. They also got me to try their festival in the town. That also made me nervous because of all of the people speaking a different language and I'd just gotten there. Although I was really surprised at how many people could talk to me.

The student decides to continue with this idea for another freewrite.

Figure 1.1.4c. Looping Sample, Part 3. This writing strategy combines multiple freewriting sessions paired with analysis and reflection.

The language barrier really scared me, but it ended up not being a big deal. My classes ~~didn't require~~ a new language, and a lot of the people in the city I stayed in spoke English anyway. At first I didn't think I would have time to learn any of their language, but I was amazed at how quickly I picked it up. There was that one time when I embarrassed myself when I tried to order the coffee and said the wrong words. The barista laughed and I'm pretty sure everyone could see how embarrassed I was.

2. Planning

After getting some early ideas in prewriting, you should stop to think about what your essay needs to say and how it will be organized. This usually means working on a thesis statement and an outline before you begin drafting.

A. Create a Strong Thesis

Every essay needs a **thesis**, a reasonable idea you have about a topic that serves as the central argument of a piece of writing. A good thesis should do two things:

1. Explain the topic (what the text is about).
2. State the claim (what you're saying about that topic).

Take a look at the following thesis statement:

> My experiences as an exchange student helped me to mature.

This thesis statement succeeds because it mentions the topic (the exchange student experience) and a claim (the experience changed the author). A great thesis also gives some idea of how the essay is arranged, as shown in the following example:

> My experiences as an exchange student helped me to mature by challenging my assumptions, expanding my comfort zone, and redefining my definition of friendship.

This thesis identifies the topic (experiences as an exchange student) and the claim (the experiences shaped the author). In addition, the reader can expect that the body of the essay will discuss assumptions, comfort zones, and friendship, likely in that order.

Try This

1. Review your assignment instructions. Determine whether the instructions require you to write about a specific topic or thesis. If the topic or thesis have already been set by your instructor, you don't need to create one.

2. If your instructions do not indicate a specific topic, you need to create your own. Start by doing some prewriting to select a topic. (Follow the sections on brainstorming, mind-mapping, freewriting, and looping.)

3. After finding a topic, decide what you want to say about that topic. Depending on the assignment, you may be required to have a specific kind of thesis. Do a freewrite to explore your opinions on the topic. Use your ideas from the freewrite to make a claim about the topic.

4. Once you've chosen a topic and a claim, combine them into a single sentence (your thesis).

5. Review your assignment instructions once more to confirm that your thesis works.

B. Create an Outline

Outlining gives your essay structure. If you create an outline during planning, you'll have a map to follow when you write a draft.

Typical outlining creates a structure of hierarchy, which means that more important ideas are placed above supporting ideas:

I.   Introduction
    A. Hook
    B. Background on topic
    C. Thesis statement
II. Body
    A. Main Idea A
        1. Support One
            a. Example A
            b. Example B
        2. Support Two
            a. Example A
            b. Example B
    B. Main Idea B
        1. Support One
            a. Example A
            b. Example B
        2. Support Two
            a. Example A
            b. Example B
    C. Main Idea C
        1. Support One
            a. Example A
            b. Example B
        2. Support Two
            a. Example A
            b. Example B
III. Conclusion
    A. Restatement of thesis
    B. Review of main ideas
    C. Parting thought

Your essays won't necessarily have a format like this example, but this example shows the idea of outline structure.

A standard rule of outlines is that if you have a 1, you must have a 2. If you have an A, you must have a B. In other words, don't break an idea into smaller ideas unless you have more than one smaller idea.

Before you can write an outline, you need to have a thesis and main ideas that support your thesis. After you've done enough prewriting to establish a thesis and some supporting ideas, you can begin to organize them with an outline (figure 1.2.1).

Try This

1. Before beginning an outline, create a clear thesis statement that satisfies your assignment instructions. (Refer to Part A above.)
2. If you haven't already done so, do a brainstorm about your thesis to list supporting ideas.
3. Group the supporting ideas that you've gathered from your brainstorming.
4. Organize the supporting ideas into an order that's easy to understand.
5. Place the organized ideas into an outline structure. Remember that primary ideas go on the top level, secondary ideas go on the subtopic level, and so on.

Figure 1.2.1. Outline Sample. Using the structure introduced in this section, this example shows how ideas can be organized into an outline.

I. Introduction
    A. Hook about an event during my trip
    B. Background on trip
    C. Thesis—how the trip changed me
    D. List main ideas: assumptions, discomfort, friendship

II. Body
    A. False assumptions
        1. Cultural traditions
        2. Language barriers
    B. Facing discomfort
        1. Trying new experiences
        2. Getting more comfortable with the unknown
        3. Wanting more new challenges
    C. New definition of friendship
        1. How the family helped me
        2. Learning to appreciate unexpected friends

III. Conclusion
    A. Restate what I learned
    B. Connect to assumptions, discomfort, and friendship
    C. Discuss the value of a study abroad experience

3. Drafting

Drafting is an early attempt to write an essay. When you draft, you probably won't create a perfect document. The purpose of drafting is to get closer to a finished essay, even if it will need more work later.

A. Use Drafts to Explore

Drafting is not freewriting. Freewriting means thinking about one or more topics before you have chosen a thesis. Drafting begins later, after you've chosen your thesis, which includes your topic and claim. Your draft should explore your thesis and develop supporting ideas.

Be flexible when drafting. Your writing may not develop as you expected. Sometimes, a draft will go in the direction that you thought it would. Other times, you'll be surprised to see something quite different. That's okay. Each project is unique, so results will vary.

Try This

1. Read your assignment instructions carefully. If you aren't sure what you're supposed to be writing, you can't complete a draft. What is the purpose of the assignment? Who is your audience (the person or people who will read your essay)?
2. Be sure you have a clear thesis in mind that indicates both a topic and a claim (what you are writing about and your opinion about it).
3. Using an outline from the planning stage can help you get started by providing a structure for the draft.
4. Write your draft, focusing on the thesis and supporting ideas. Try to write quickly without stopping to fix things. (You can change the details later.)
5. If your assignment has a required number of words or pages, try to write at least as much as the minimum. In general, it's better to write more than the minimum in a draft.

B. Make Multiple Drafts

Many students think that only one draft is needed. The truth is that most writers need multiple drafts to communicate clearly. In most cases, early drafts are warm-ups. Drafting is like the pregame in a sport, when the players get their minds and bodies engaged. Drafting is also like those practice notes that musicians play in preparation before a concert. You should draft at the beginning to get into a rhythm and a sense of what you are trying to say.

Try This

1. When your draft is complete, review your instructions once more.
2. Now read your draft, slowly. For the best results, read aloud.
3. After reading the draft, consider what could be better. What are you missing? Did you accomplish the purpose of the assignment? Did you write for the correct audience?
4. If the draft isn't doing everything required by the assignment, do another draft.
5. Repeat these steps as many times as needed.
6. Consult your campus Writing or Tutoring Center for further feedback

4. Revising

Revision focuses on an entire essay. Revision is not about the small, sentence-level questions that relate to writing conventions (things like grammar, punctuation, or word choice). Instead, revision focuses on the big picture. Consider the how your thesis connects the different parts of the essay. What are you trying to say as a whole in the essay? If you look at the entire essay and think about how it works, you can begin to make the essay clearer for the reader.

Think for a moment about the word *revision*. It's made of two parts: *re-* plus *vision*. *Re-* means "again." *Vision* comes from the Latin word for "to see." So in one sense, *revision* means, "to see again." This little word history can be helpful as you think about your job during revision. Try to see what you wrote as if you haven't read it before.

A. Find Your Focus

When revising, you will usually find that while parts of your essay are good, other parts don't fit your goal or the requirements of the assignment. Perhaps the essay wanders from your topic. Perhaps the connection to your thesis isn't clear in some sections. Your task during revision is to improve the parts of the essay that lack a clear connection to the rest of the essay. You may think that everything you wrote is perfect, but most drafts have sections that need improvement or simply don't belong in the essay.

Try This

1. Read through your draft. As you read, mark any sections that seem to repeat an idea or deal with a concept that doesn't fit. Think about your thesis as you do this. If the relationship between the thesis and the idea of the section isn't clear, mark the section.
2. After reading and marking the draft, go back and improve the sections you marked. If sections are too long, make them shorter. If sections aren't needed at all, eliminate them.
3. Review your draft again. This time you shouldn't have sections that repeat the same idea or wander off topic. If you do, repeat the process.

B. Question Everything

Carefully consider how you have communicated. Question everything that you've written. Read your draft like a first-time reader. Imagine that you know nothing about your essay. Would you understand the purpose of the essay? Is the thesis clear? Does every part of the work relate to that thesis? Answer these questions honestly as you review the draft.

Try This

1. Review your draft. As you read, mark any section in which you are being unclear. Think about the following questions:
   a. Will the reader need prior knowledge to understand the topic?
   b. Does the text include words the reader may not know?
   c. Does the text use terms in an unusual way?
   d. Does the text take things for granted that need to be explained?
   e. Do parts of the text have an unclear connection to the thesis?
2. If the answer to any of the questions is yes, mark the section.
3. When you're done reading, go back and review the sections you marked. Consider how to fix those sections. Your options are:
   a. Revise to improve the section.
   b. Remove the section.
4. After making changes, review your draft again to confirm that the sections make sense and that you don't need to make further changes.

C. Create a Reverse Outline

A standard outline is created during prewriting and offers a structure for your drafting to follow. In a **reverse outline**, you do the opposite. You start with a draft and then create an outline based on that draft. Then you can use the reverse outline to help you think about ways to improve your draft.

Try This

1. Count the number of paragraphs in your draft.
2. On a new sheet of paper, list the numbers.
3. For each number, write two things about that paragraph in your draft:
   a. What is the paragraph about? (In other words, what does it say?)
   b. What is the paragraph doing? (In other words, what is its purpose?)
4. After you've written both what the paragraph says and what it does, you'll have a complete reverse outline. Ask yourself the following questions based on your reverse outline.
   a. Does the draft repeat ideas? Do any of the paragraphs say the same thing?
   b. Is the draft missing anything? Do any important ideas need to be added to paragraphs?
   c. Is the draft accomplishing its intended purpose? Do paragraphs support the thesis? Do any paragraphs make it harder to understand the purpose?
   d. Is the draft organized? Do any paragraphs need to move?

5. Editing

The last stage in the writing process is **editing**, which is improving the small, sentence-level details. Never skip this step. Allow time to edit before you submit an assignment, because it will make a difference in your grade.

Unlike revision, which looks at how parts fit into an entire essay, editing focuses on the details. If you've done a good job with your revision, you can stop thinking about your thesis, main ideas, paragraphs, and other big picture elements.

Most of what you should focus on during editing are what instructors call the writing **conventions**. These are things such as grammar, punctuation, spelling, capitalization, and other common expectations. See the Top 10 Issues section to review the most common problems that students miss when editing.

You've probably used a number of editing approaches. Here are several you should try.

A. Read Aloud

This may sound like a waste of time (or a little silly), but reading your essays aloud can help you catch editing issues. You've probably had the experience of writing the same word twice and not catching it. This happens frequently, and it's easy to miss when you only read your essay in your head. If you read aloud, you'll often catch mistakes that your eye might skip over.

Try This

1. Find a device with a voice recording feature. (Most phones have this ability, as well as the majority of tablets and laptops.)
2. Record yourself reading your essay.
3. After you're done reading your essay, play the recording. Listen carefully for issues.
4. When you notice an editing issue, pause the recording to fix the problem in your essay.
5. Continue playing the recording and work through the rest of the essay.

B. Change the Appearance

If you wrote your essay electronically, try printing it out when you edit. Simply changing the way an essay looks can help you to catch problems when editing. This might seem like a waste of paper, but you'll likely find a couple of issues that you missed when looking at a digital copy. If you're editing on a screen, try changing the appearance.

Try This

1. Change the font style. Do this by opening your essay in a word processor, selecting all of the text, and picking a new appearance for the letters.
2. Read the entire essay in this new font. The different look will cause you to slow down and notice what you wrote.
3. Next, increase the font size and read again. Changing your font to a larger size might help you to catch issues that you missed. Make the font large enough to increase the overall length of the document. This will make it easier to see errors in punctuation, formatting, and repeated words.
4. Be sure to switch your font back to an appropriate choice before submitting your assignment. Check with your instructor if you're not sure about the preference.

C. Use a Handbook

You probably have a writing handbook for your current or past composition classes. These handbooks explain conventions (standards like grammar and punctuation), formatting (how documents look on a page), and academic styles (specific ways to arrange a document and talk about sources). Use a handbook when you edit. If you're not familiar with conventions like fragments or commas, look them up. The internet can also be helpful in this area, although you should look for quality academic sources to help you, such as the Purdue OWL.

When you edit, check your formatting and style using a handbook. Most writing classes require you to use a certain academic style, such as MLA (short for Modern Language Association) or APA (short for American Psychological Association). These styles give writers guidelines for using sources and arranging the format of a document.

Even if your class doesn't use one of these styles, your instructor will have requirements about how your essays should look. Carefully review your class syllabus, the assignment description, and any other guides that have been provided in class or online. Be sure that you're satisfying your instructor's expectations for things like page numbers, headings, and titles.

If you've used any sources, you need to edit your citations. A **citation** is a way of giving credit to the sources that you use in an essay. The information you need to include for a citation will vary depending on the academic style, so follow a handbook. (To make the citation process easier, keep track of your sources as you draft and revise.) When editing your citations, check that you've done the following:

1. Mention the name of the authors and/or works in the body of the essay.
2. List the full source information for those borrowed works in the required location (usually at the end of the essay).
3. Confirm that you've given credit for all borrowed information, whether directly quoted or put into your own words.

Try This

Open a writing handbook to a sample essay in the academic style required by your class. Compare your essay to the sample. Check the essay for the following items:
- [ ] Class information (names, class, date)
- [ ] Page header (the information at the top of the page—the content varies by style)
- [ ] Title
- [ ] Margins
- [ ] Line spacing
- [ ] Paragraph indents (the empty space before the first line)
- [ ] Sources page

D. Get Help

While it's your job to edit your work, there's nothing wrong with getting extra help with editing. In fact, an extra set of eyes can make a big difference after you've done your best to catch everything. If you have a classmate, friend, or family member who will review your finished work, try to get their help on every essay. Be sure they understand basic writing conventions such as grammar, punctuation, and capitalization. Also, don't forget to thank anyone who helps you.

Try This

1. If your essay needs more editing, give it time. Taking a break can make a difference.
2. Set aside the essay for a day and focus on other activities. At minimum, give yourself a break for an hour or two.
3. Try getting some exercise or a change of environment. Maybe go for a walk or do some work around the house.
4. When you return to the essay after your break, you will notice things that you missed.

Part 2

Essay Structure

Using good structure makes your writing easy to understand. One of your jobs as a writer is to guide your readers. By having clear paragraph structure, you help the reader easily move through your text.

Always review assignment instructions for specifics about essay structure. While you may not always be given requirements about the arrangement of your essay, some instructors have certain expectations. In general, follow the principles about paragraph and sentence structure explained below.

1. Building Paragraphs

A **paragraph** is a group of sentences with a shared idea.

A. Include Only One Main Idea in Each Paragraph

Do not put multiple main ideas in the same paragraph. If you need to break a main idea into supporting ideas, that's fine. However, you should put the supporting ideas into separate paragraphs. Take a look at the following paragraph to see if you can identify its main idea:

When I was studying abroad, I realized that my assumptions about other cultures were wrong. I experienced fascinating customs and traditions. I also noticed that I was frightened of trying new things, so I had to get over that. I gained a new friend who loved art more than sports. I'm excited to visit even more places to learn about additional cultures.

This paragraph combines too many ideas. The result is confusing. Each of these concepts needs at least one paragraph.

B. Write Multiple Paragraphs

By using more than one paragraph, you can clarify main ideas and keep them separate. Occasionally, you'll be asked to write an essay in a single paragraph. For most assignments, however, you are expected to use multiple paragraphs. If you write an entire essay using only one, your ideas will likely seem crowded and confusing to readers.

Notice how the idea from the first example is developed over multiple paragraphs:

The months I spent in another country exposed my inaccurate ideas about the culture of other countries. I'd always thought of the culture of other countries as strange, but what I experienced when I studied abroad changed my mind. I discovered that I loved experiencing new cultures. I learned many things about art and history. I experienced fascinating customs and traditions. As a result, I am excited to visit even more places to learn about additional cultures.

While I was aware of my assumptions before going abroad, I didn't realize that my comfort zone needed to expand. Once I was in a new environment, I soon noticed that I was frightened of trying new things. Thankfully, my host family encouraged me to keep having new experiences. As a result of their efforts, I gradually changed my view on unfamiliar things. Instead of fearing things I haven't tried, I'm now excited about doing new things.

Perhaps the most important way that I matured was my view of friendship. My year abroad showed me that friends can have different interests. As an athlete, I wasn't previously interested in being friends with people my age who didn't like sports. While I was studying abroad, the girl who became my closest friend had no interest in sports. Instead, she loved animals and art. After we became friends, she helped me to understand why she loved those things so much. This has helped me realize that I can be friends with people who don't share all of my interests. As a result, I've gained many new friends since returning home, and I've learned about many things I didn't know before.

Giving each of these ideas a separate paragraph allows them to be understood one at a time. This version also allowed the writer to go into some detail and offer examples.

C. Connect Paragraphs to Your Thesis

Your paragraphs must relate to your thesis. Remember, your thesis identifies the topic and your claim about the topic. Here's an example of a thesis statement from earlier:

> My experiences as an exchange student helped me to mature by challenging my assumptions, expanding my comfort zone, and redefining my definition of friendship.

Every sentence and paragraph you write must clearly connect back to the thesis. The reader should never wonder, "How does this relate to the point of the essay?" Notice how the following example connects to the main idea without exact repetition of the thesis:

> My time abroad showed me that some of my views about other cultures were immature.

This sentence explains how the paragraph regarding assumptions relates back to the overall thesis of studying abroad and maturation.

D. Develop Opening and Closing Paragraphs

Unless you've been instructed otherwise, always include an introduction in the form of an opening paragraph and a conclusion in the form of a final paragraph. If an assignment calls for a single paragraph, include a sentence or two of introduction and conclusion. Most of the time, you'll need a separate paragraph for each.

A strong introduction should do the following:

1. Get the reader's attention.
2. Introduce the topic.
3. Provide some details.
4. State your thesis.
5. Provide some sense of the main ideas and organization.

See if you can identify the elements of a strong introduction in the following example:

> Growing up, the idea of leaving my family and home to live in another country scared me. Still, I made the surprising decision to be a foreign exchange student during my senior year of high school. This turned out to be one of the best choices I've ever made. My experiences as an exchange student helped me to mature by challenging my assumptions, expanding my comfort zone, and improving my understanding of friendship.

Notice that the writer gets the reader's attention by emphasizing change (a before and after). The writer also introduces the topic (studying abroad), adds details about the background of their experience, states their thesis, and mentions the main ideas.

A strong conclusion should do the following:

1. Review the thesis.
2. Review the main ideas.
3. Leave the reader with a parting thought (such as a call to action, a prediction, or an interesting connection).

Look for the elements of a strong conclusion in the following example:

> I'll always be glad that I chose to be an exchange student. As a result of the experience, I believe I've become a better person. My understanding of other cultures, my comfort zone, and friendship were all challenged and reshaped. If I hadn't completed the program, I would have remained a sheltered person with much narrower views. I recommend studying abroad to anyone who has the opportunity. The experience is truly life-changing.

This conclusion succeeds because in reinforces the author's claim about the topic, reviews what was significant about the main ideas, and offers something for the reader to think about at the end.

2. Connecting Sentences

Use sentences to show the main idea of paragraphs, add details to those ideas, and clarify the relationship between different paragraphs.

A. Include Topic Sentences

One sentence should clearly explain the main idea of the paragraph. This sentence typically appears near the beginning of the paragraph and is called the topic sentence.

If you read only the first sentence in the following example, you should have a good idea what its topic will be:

> The months I spent in another country taught me the joy of learning about other cultures. I'd always thought of the culture of other countries as strange, but what I experienced when I studied abroad changed my mind. I discovered that I loved experiencing new cultures. I learned many things about art and history. I experienced fascinating customs and traditions. As a result, I am excited to visit even more places to learn about additional cultures.

A good topic sentence allows the reader to understand what the paragraph is about and how it relates to the bigger picture. A great topic sentence also indicates some of the structure in a paragraph by mentioning some of the details.

B. Develop Supporting Sentences

While paragraphs occasionally consist of a single sentence, a typical paragraph will have several in addition to the topic sentence. A supporting sentence develops the main idea of the paragraph by offering more information and details. The supporting sentences in the following example build on the idea presented in the topic sentence:

> The months I spent in another country taught me the joy of learning about other cultures. I'd always thought of the culture of other countries as strange, but what I experienced when I studied abroad changed my mind. I discovered that I loved experiencing new cultures. I learned many things about art and history. I experienced fascinating customs and traditions. As a result, I am excited to visit even more places to learn about additional cultures.

While the topic sentence at the beginning of this paragraph makes the main idea clear, the additional sentences offer more information to expand on the same idea.

C. Add Transitions

Readers must work hard to understand a text. Help them by providing appropriate transitions, words that explain the relationship of a paragraph to the one that came before it. A good paragraph transitions smoothly into the paragraph that comes after it, as well. In the following example, the first part of the sentence connects to the writer's growing awareness, and the second part of the sentence points to the writer's need to keep growing:

> While I was aware of my assumptions before going abroad, I didn't realize that my comfort zone needed to expand.

This sentence would be an effective way to transition from one body paragraph to the next. It succeeds because it connects one main idea to the next main idea.

3. Finding Useful Models

A. Sample Student Essay

Read through this essay by Chemeketa Community College student Kevin Anderson. Think about where this essay uses structure well and where it could use some improvement. Use the notes to help you. For more essay examples and practice, refer to the appendix at the end of the book.

Figure 2.3.1a. Student Essay Sample. Page 1.

> The title reflects the author's content rather than the assignment and is centered on the page, without any additional formatting.

> Most introductions begin with a fact or detail about the topic, add background information, and conclude with the thesis statement.

> A thesis statement states a topic and a detail or position (opinion) on that topic. It is typically located at the end of the introduction.

> Each body paragraph begins with a topic sentence that explain the main idea of the paragraph and connects back to the thesis.

> Body paragraphs support the thesis with details and examples.

Student 1

Kevin Anderson

Professor Cortes

WR090

24 November 2021

Procrastination and Pushing Through to One's Goals

The urge to do something fun or relaxing instead of a tedious task is a familiar feeling to students. Making the choice between playing math or video games, reading a chapter of a textbook versus a good science fiction novel, or watching a movie instead of a lecture is a well-known struggle. While there will always be distractions and excuses to avoid doing things one is not enthusiastic about, there are many strategies that provide ways to overcome procrastination. I believe it is possible to use a positive mindset and reliable goal-setting strategies to push through procrastination and into success.

One of the main reasons people procrastinate is a lack of motivation to accomplish the task due to it appearing boring, repetitive, or unpleasant in comparison to a recreational activity or another task. In a Ted Talk given by Tim Urban entitled "Inside the Mind of a Master Procrastinator," this situation is well described. Urban explains, "There is a difference [between 'normal' brains and those of procrastinators]. Both brains have a Rational Decision-Maker in them, but the procrastinator's brain also has an Instant Gratification Monkey" (Urban 00:03:47–55). Urban explains the Instant Gratification Monkey is the part of the brain that seeks out activities and tasks that are

Figure 2.3.1b. Student Essay Sample. Page 2.

fun and immediate and avoids anything else. I feel this is an accurate description of the struggle one experiences with the urge to procrastinate. Instead of focusing on avoiding procrastinating, finding ways to overcome procrastination can be easier and more effective overall.

Accordingly, having a positive mindset is a useful tool in overcoming procrastination. In my own experience, looking past the parts of a task that are not enjoyable or finding an enjoyable part is a way to develop positive thoughts about the task. Finding that fun can be a way to avoid the urge to look for fun elsewhere and accomplish the task. Making the task a game can also bring that positivity into play. Seeing how many practice questions for a test one can answer correctly in a row, attempting to complete a household chore faster than previously done, or having a minor competition with a colleague are all ways to bring some positivity into play. These are just examples of ways to bring more of a positive mindset to a potentially boring task.

Focusing on what one can gain from accomplishing a task is also a way to reframe the thought process that can lead to motivation to complete the task. Thinking about the reward can be an easy way to make a task seem less unpleasant. Whether the task is a household chore, a part of one's job that is not enjoyable, or an academic activity, focusing on the reward at the end provides motivation to accomplish the task. In his article entitled "Procrastination: Beating the Big Put-Off," Victor Parachin talks about how a reward system can be very helpful in overcoming procrastination, stating that "rewarding movement and progress rather than criticizing yourself for setbacks will

> Each body paragraph includes a closing statement which reminds the reader of the main idea or hints at the content to come.

> Outside sources should be framed when included. An introductory phrase or sentence typically appears before a quotation.

Figure 2.3.1c. Student Essay Sample. Page 3.

encourage continued advance" (20). If one needs to read a book that is not very interesting to them, set a gummy bear, or some other small enjoyable treat, at the end of each page or section. Complete that section and earn a small reward. Parachin also states, "Don't diminish your accomplishments by thinking they are not worth the rewards you set aside for them," (20) which is a clear statement of how rewards can not only motivate but also validate the accomplishments one makes. Feeling that validation will not only help maintain positivity but encourage further efforts to accomplish more.

Recognizing those accomplishments can be very productive toward building a more lasting positive mindset regarding pushing through procrastination. To make recognition of progress more attainable, clear and achievable goal setting is an invaluable tool. Parachin also speaks of the importance of making goals achievable, explaining that "unrealistic goals lead to quick discouragement and easy defeat" (19). Parachin follows that statement up with an explanation of how to best utilize goal-setting to be productive: "Success comes from using small, daily goals to reach big, long-range ones" (19). Taking a task that may seem daunting, if not impossible, and breaking it down into smaller, more achievable goals can be very beneficial. It helps prevent being intimidated by the task, which can lead to procrastination before even beginning, and makes completing each step its own accomplishment, which leads to additional motivation to move forward. As more tasks are finished, the initially overwhelming task is closer to completion and motivation continues to build throughout.

Quotations and paraphrases should be explained or commented upon to connect them to the rest of the essay.

Sources need to be cited using the style required by the particular class. Style handbooks demonstrate the process.

Figure 2.3.1d. Student Essay Sample. Page 4.

Student 4

While procrastination can be quite a challenge to overcome, especially if it has been something one has struggled with for most of their life, becoming less of a procrastinator is still possible. As Parachin states, "Even if you've been a procrastinator all your life, that way of living can be totally changed. In dealing with procrastination you're taking charge of your life at a higher level. As you do that, you will experience more fulfilling, happy results, and accomplishments" (20). To me, that is the core of why pushing through procrastination is such an important goal. Breaking out of the cycle of procrastination and achieving one's goals will increase not only productivity but feelings of accomplishment and fulfillment in life.

Transitional words and phrases show readers the relationship between ideas, sentences, and paragraphs.

The concluding paragraph signals the end of the essay, reminds the reader of the thesis, and ends with a parting thought.

Figure 2.3.1e. Student Essay Sample. Page 5.

A citation page at the end of an essay is used if outside sources are quoted or paraphrased.

Student 5

Works Cited

Parachin, Victor. "Procrastination: Beating the Big Put-Off." *Listen*, vol. 51, no. 10, Oct.

1998, pp. 18–20. *ProQuest*, www-proquest-

com.chemeketa.idm.oclc.org/docview/

230510281/fulltextPDF/. PDF download.

Urban, Tim. "Inside the Mind of a Master Procrastinator." *TED*, Feb. 2016,

www.ted.com/talks/tim_urban_inside_the_mind_of_a_master_procrastinator.

Part 3

Top Ten Issues

Part 3 introduces ten of the most common problems in student writing. These specific issues have been selected because they often appear in essays. Review the concepts and practice them until they are natural.

Why do these issues matter? Aren't they just a way for writing instructors to make your life complicated? Actually, editing and "correctness" in writing is about making your communication easier to understand. The rules for writing conventions help to establish a common approach. When writers follow a similar set of rules in areas such as grammar or punctuation, readers have an easier time understanding what is being communicated.

1. Fragments

A **fragment** is an incomplete sentence. You can fix a fragment by adding additional information to the sentence.

Complete Sentences: Avoiding Fragments
Every sentence must:

1. Have a subject
2. Have a verb
3. Be a complete thought

Fragments occur when at least one of these elements is missing:
1. There is no subject
2. There is no main verb:
   » -ing ending verbs do not work as the main verb
   » To + verb (infinitives) do not work as the main verb
3. There is no complete thought:
   » Dependent clause
   » The main clause (subject + verb) is missing completely

Fragment Fixes
1. Replace:
   » Add the missing subject or verb
2. Remove:
   » Take out the dependent word or phrase causing the fragment
3. Join:
   » Combine the fragment with the sentence before or after it, if it makes sense to do so.

A. Explanation and Examples
To understand fragments, you first must understand the basic parts of a sentence.

1. Complete Sentences
Every sentence must have three parts:

1. A subject
2. A verb
3. A complete thought

Let's review these parts:

A **subject** is the thing doing something in a sentence. It's a person, animal, or object that acts. In English, the subject is often located at the beginning of the sentence.

> The student found the classroom. (Correct)

A **verb** is the action or existence in the sentence. The subject *does* the verb.

> The student found the classroom. (Correct)

A complete thought is enough words for a sentence to make sense by itself. The sentence must be clear even if it is read on its own.

> The student found the classroom. (Correct)

The entire sentence shares a complete thought—nothing is missing.

2. Incomplete Sentences

A sentence fragment happens when one or more of the required parts (subject, verb, complete thought) are missing.

> Found. (Incorrect)

Wait, *who* found? This is a fragment because it lacks a subject.

> The student. (Incorrect)

What about the student? What is the student doing? This is a fragment because it's missing a verb.

The student found. (Incorrect)

This is close, but it's still a fragment because it doesn't have a complete thought. What is the student finding? When readers see the word *found*, they expect a word for the thing being discovered.

The student found the classroom. (Correct)

Now we have all three elements together. The subject, verb, and complete thought are present, making this a complete sentence.

B. More Examples

As you look at each of the incorrect versions below, try to identify what is wrong. Then try to think of a way to fix it. Use the corrected version to help you understand the issue and how to correct it.

The following sentence lacks a subject: Who is at the library? It also lacks a verb: What is happening?

> While at the library. (Incorrect)

This sentence is not a complete thought: While at the library, what? By answering those questions, you can arrive at a complete thought.

> While at the library, I used a computer to find research articles. (Correct)

See if you can identify what's missing in the following example:

> The group members planned their presentation. Planned for hours. (Incorrect)

The first sentence in this example is complete. The second sentence—while it has great style—is a fragment. It needs a subject.

> The group members planned their presentation. They planned for hours. (Correct)

See *Your Guide to College Writing* (Chemeketa Press 2021) for additional examples: pp. 32–33 and pp. 66–70.

C. Practice

Test your understanding by fixing these examples. We've helped you with the first few.

1. The large number of textbooks.

This sentence lacks a verb and a complete thought. Fix it by providing a verb for the word *textbooks* and making a complete thought.

_____

2. So complicated!

This sentence lacks a subject and a verb. Provide both and be sure that the sentence is a complete thought.

_____

3. Read for two hours.

This sentence needs a subject. Add a subject to make the sentence complete.

_____

4. Even when it's early in the school term.

Don't be fooled. This sentence doesn't have a complete thought. The reader thinks, "Even when it's early in the school term, what?" Add to the sentence to make it a complete thought.

_____

5. The desk that was made by my uncle.

---

6. Walking across campus.

---

7. Difficult to complete in three days.

---

8. Once the study session was over.

---

9. While visiting the IT department.

---

10. Across from the coffee shop.

---

2. Run-On Sentences

A **run-on sentence** is multiple sentences combined into one. You can fix a run-on sentence by joining sentences correctly or by separating them.

Correcting Run-on Sentences

One goal for good academic writing is sentence variety, so choosing different ways to fix run-ons is helpful.

Option 1: Period and Capital Letter
Independent clause. Independent clause.

Option 2: Comma Plus Coordinating Conjunction (FANBOYS)
Independent clause, <u>or</u> independent clause.

Option 3: Semicolon
Independent clause; independent clause.

Option 4: Semicolon and Conjunctive Adverb (Joining Word or Phrase)
Independent clause; <u>however</u>, independent clause

Common Conjunctive Adverbs
Typically a conjunctive adverb is followed by a comma, but some exceptions are included in the list below.

accordingly,	furthermore,	namely,
also,	further,	nevertheless,
as a result,	however,	of course,
besides,	in addition,	on the other hand,
certainly,	in fact,	similarly,
consequently,	instead,	then
finally,	likewise,	therefore,
for example,	meanwhile,	thus

Option 5: Dependent Word or Phrase
This option effectively changes one of the two independent phrases into a fragment, allowing the independent and dependent phrases to be joined together.

Method 1: Because dependent clause, independent clause.
If a dependent word or phrase begins the sentence, the phrase is followed by a
   comma. (This is the same as an introductory element use of a comma.)

Method 2: Independent clause because dependent clause.
If the dependent phrase comes at the end of the sentence, the dependent word
   or phrase is placed between the two clauses, generally without a comma.

Common Dependent Words and Phrases

although	once	until
as	since	when
as though	so that	whenever
because	that	where
before	though	which
if	unless	while

A. Explanation and Examples

To understand run-on sentences, you first must understand the basic parts of a complete
sentence.

1. Complete Sentences

Every sentence must have three parts:

4. A subject
5. A verb
6. A complete thought

   Let's review these parts:

A subject is the thing doing something in a sentence. It's a person, animal, or object that
acts.

The instructor brought snacks. (Correct)

A verb is the action or existence in the sentence. The subject does the verb.

The instructor brought snacks. (Correct)

A complete thought is enough words for a sentence to make sense by itself. The sentence must be clear even if it were read alone.

> The instructor brought snacks. (Correct)

The entire sentence expresses a complete thought—nothing is missing.

2. Run-Ons

As mentioned earlier, a run-on sentence happens when two or more complete sentences are not joined correctly.

> The instructor brought snacks everyone was happy. (Incorrect)

This is a run-on because these are two complete sentences. They need to be joined correctly, rather than simply run together.

Complete sentences can be joined in the following three ways:

1. A period (.)
2. A semicolon (;)
3. A comma (,) + a **coordinating conjunction** (*for, and, nor, but, or, yet, so*)

Using a period to separate two complete sentences is one way to fix a run-on. This method is always appropriate.

> The instructor brought snacks. Everyone was happy. (Correct)

Another way to join complete sentences is to use a semicolon to separate the two ideas. The sentence that comes after the semicolon should show that something is being added to the idea of the first sentence.

> The whole class enjoyed the snacks; even that grumpy student liked it. (Correct)

A third way to fix a run-on sentence is to combine the two sentences using *both* a comma and a coordinating conjunction.

> The instructor brought snacks, and everyone was happy. (Correct)

If you struggle to remember the coordinating conjunctions, just think of the acronym **FANBOYS**:

For	And	Nor	But	Or	Yet	So

3. Comma Splices

When you join two complete sentences with just a comma, this creates a type of run-on sentence known as a **comma splice**.

> The instructor brought snacks, everyone was happy. (Incorrect)

To fix a comma splice, add a coordinating conjunction (FANBOYS) after the comma.

> The instructor brought snacks, so everyone was happy. (Correct)

B. More Examples

As you look at each of the incorrect versions below, try to identify what is wrong. Then try to think of a way to fix it. Use the corrected version to help you understand the issue and how to correct it.

Read the following sentence and try to find where exactly it becomes a run-on sentence:

> My class has reading assignments they are usually long. (Incorrect)

In this example, a period has been added to make two complete sentences.

My class has reading assignments. They are usually long. (Correct)

The same sentence can be combined into a compound sentence using a semicolon.

My class has reading assignments; they are usually long. (Correct)

Another option is to separate the two complete sentences with a comma and a coordinating conjunction.

My class has reading assignments, and they are usually long. (Correct)

See if you can find where exactly the following example becomes a run-on sentence:

Don't forget to get a good night's sleep it makes a difference. (Incorrect)

In this example, a period has been added to make two complete sentences.

Don't forget to get a good night's sleep. It makes a difference. (Correct)

The same sentence can be combined into a compound sentence using a semicolon.

Don't forget to get a good night's sleep; it makes a difference. (Correct)

C. Practice

Test your understanding by fixing these examples. We've helped you with the first few.

> 1. My sister says math is her favorite class she thinks it's easy.

This sentence is a run-on because two complete sentences are fused together. Fix it by using one of the three methods (a period, a semicolon, or a comma and coordinating conjunction).

> 2. The rain keeps pouring, I'm glad to be inside the building.

This sentence is a comma splice because two complete sentences are joined with only a comma. Fix it by adding a coordinating conjunction to the comma. Alternatively, you could use a period or semicolon.

> 3. Yesterday was encouraging I hope today will also be good.

This sentence is a run-on because two complete sentences are fused together. Fix it by using one of the three methods (a period, a semicolon, or a comma and coordinating conjunction).

> 4. The days grow shorter and fall is just around the corner.

This sentence is a run-on because two sentences are joined incorrectly. While we have a coordinating conjunction (and), we still need a comma. We could also use a period or semicolon.

---

5. Never skip your reading assignments, always complete them.

_____

6. Kyle prefers mechanical pencils, he uses them for note-taking.

_____

7. I was hungry I was angry I was tired.

_____

8. No topics had come to mind, nothing had occurred to my team members.

_____

9. Sometimes my friend rides with me to school, she always meets me at the same spot.

_____

10. The problem with the bus couldn't be fixed it needed to be replaced.

_____

3. Verb Tenses

Verb tenses show when something happens. Be consistent and use verb tense correctly to help readers understand.

A. Explanation and Examples

A **verb** is a word that shows action or state of being, and it can change depending on when something is happening in the sentence. The form of the verb that shows this is called the verb tense.

There are three basic verb tenses:

1. **Past:** The student researched.
2. **Present:** The student researches.
3. **Future:** The student will research.

Two common problems in student writing are switching tenses and using the wrong tense for the context.

1. Tense Switching

Tense switching happens when a writer changes verb tense incorrectly in a single context. Keep your verb tenses in the same tense unless you need to reflect a shift in time.

> I researched in the library, and then I write my essay. (Incorrect)

Notice that the main verb (researched) is in past tense, then it shifts to present. The verb should have stayed in past tense.

> I researched in the library, and then I wrote my essay. (Correct)

2. Wrong Tense

Use the correct verb tense for your situation. For a narrative, use past tense. When you introduce a quote by someone else, called an **attribution**, use present tense.

When you describe events in a narrative (a retelling of what happened), use past tense for the main verb.

> My high school teachers showed me the importance of quality research.
> (Correct)

When you quote a writer, keep the attribution verb in present tense. This can sometimes seem odd when the writer did their communicating in the past, as shown in the following example:

> Shakespeare says, "Parting is such sweet sorrow." (Correct)

Notice that we write "Shakespeare says," not "Shakespeare said." This can be confusing, because in a history class, you would refer to Shakespeare in the past tense.

> Shakespeare wrote his plays during the Elizabethan Era. (Correct)

In this case, we use past tense because we're describing what the author did from a historical perspective.

On the other hand, when we quote an author or discuss the meaning of their writing, we use present tense. The idea is that the author's thinking is continuing to the present.

> Shakespeare presents Macbeth as a human deeply troubled by the result of his choices. (Correct)

Don't confuse the difference between the attribution (the verb describing the author's actions) and the actual quotation or summary of a source. Often, the quotation or summary will be in past tense.

> Wilson states that most of the data resulted from experiments. (Correct)

The author attribution is in present tense. The summary is in past tense.

B. More Examples

As you look at each of the incorrect versions below, try to identify what is wrong. Then try to think of a way to fix it. Use the corrected version to help you understand the issue and how to correct it.

Compare the verbs in the following example:

> Students completed research about the topic the teacher assigns. (Incorrect)

The sentence begins in past tense, so it should continue in past tense.

> Students completed research about the topic the teacher assigned. (Correct)

Compare the verbs in the following example:

> The librarians shelved books that students return. (Incorrect)

The following sentence begins in past tense, so it should continue in past tense.

> The librarians shelved books that students returned. (Correct)

Compare the verbs in the following example:

> In *Make College Yours*, Liss shared stories about students who overcome difficulties. (Incorrect)

The following example uses present tense to describe the work of the author, and uses past tense for events in the work.

> In *Make College Yours*, Liss shares stories about students who overcame difficulties. (Correct)

C. Practice

Test your understanding by fixing these examples. We've helped you with the first few.

1. Most student clubs **are** more topical than competitive. Some **were** narrowly focused.

(The verb tense needs to stay the same. Use present tense when describing things that continue to be true.)

_____

2. Groups like Phi Theta Kappa accept members who **achieve** and **maintained** a certain GPA.

(The verb tense needs to stay the same.)

_____

3. Student government **will be** a campus group that **played** an important role in the college.

(The verb tense needs to stay the same.)

_____

4. Student government **is** intentionally **organized** to **have included** as many campus voices as possible.

(The verb tense needs to stay the same.)

_____

5. **Talk** to your college's outreach faculty and staff **to have gotten** suggestions for places that might benefit from your talents.

_____

Use the correct verb tense for the writing context.

6. Eric Hoffer **said**, "It is the true learners who inherit the future."

_____

7. Covey **insisted** that priorities are the most important part of time management.

_____

8. In *Great Expectations*, Dickens **described** the character of Miss Havisham as a strange, reclusive spinster.

_____

9. The character named Pip in *Great Expectations* **wants** to be in a romantic relationship with Estella.

_____

10. Able Magwitch is the criminal in *Great Expectations* who remembers Pip's kindness to him.

_____

4. Subject-Verb Agreement

Subject-verb agreement means that the subject and verb in a sentence match.

A. Explanation and Examples

Subjects and verbs must agree in number. This means that a singular subject must pair with a singular verb.

> The girl studies her lesson. (Correct)

Girl is a singular subject. *Studies* is a singular verb. The subject and verb agree in this sentence. English verbs often have an *s* at the end when they are singular, but not when they are plural—it's the opposite of the nouns.

A plural subject goes with a plural verb.

> The girls study their lesson. (Correct)

We run into problems when the subject and verb don't match. In the following example, the plural subject *girls* is incorrectly paired with a singular verb.

> The girls studies their lesson. (Incorrect)

Short sentences like this are easier to catch. Longer sentences—especially when other words come between the subject and verb—are easier to miss.

> The girls who live together in the same apartment studies their lesson. (Incorrect)

In this sentence, it might be easy to miss that *girls* is a plural subject and that *studies* needs to be plural.

1. Compound Subjects

Don't be fooled if a sentence has a compound subject, which means there is more than one subject. Because we have two subjects in this sentence, the sentence needs a plural verb.

> The girl and her friend study for their lesson. (Correct)

This is true even though, individually, the nouns *girl* and *friend* are singular.

2. Compound Verbs

The same principle is true if a sentence has a compound verb, which means there is more than one action.

> The girl studies and reviews her lesson. (Correct)

Even though this sentence has two verbs, they remain singular because the subject *girl* is singular.

B. More Examples

As you look at each of the incorrect versions below, try to identify what is wrong. Then try to think of a way to fix it. Use the corrected version to help you understand the issue and how to correct it.

Check to see if the subjects and the verb match in the following example:

> The student and professor talks during the office hour. (Incorrect)

The sentence has a compound subject, so it needs a plural verb.

> The student and professor talk during the office hour. (Correct)

Check to see if the subject and the verbs match in the following example:

> A research librarian locates and recommend sources. (Incorrect)

The compound verbs must match the singular subject.

> A research librarian locates and recommends sources. (Correct)

C. Practice

Test your understanding by fixing these examples. We've helped you with the first few.

1. The culture of college assumes that a student's number one priority **are** academic study.

(The verb *are* needs to match the subject *priority*.)

2. The culture of college **expect** you to do your own work and to be honest in your interactions with others.

(The verb *expect* needs to match the subject *culture*.)

3. Academic integrity **mean** doing your own work.

(The verb *mean* needs to match the subject *integrity*.)

4. Sometimes, your best effort may seem way more than what **are** needed.

(The verb *are* needs to match the subject *effort*.)

5. Generating your own questions **are** ideal.

6. Many student organizations **showcases** what they have to offer through club fairs and information sessions.

7. Student government **are** a great place for people who want to help make the college experience a supportive, enriching experience.

8. Your campus multicultural center **have** access to dates, times, and locations for many of them.

9. A student of history **read** a lot of books.

10. Completing exams, along with assignments, **require** organization.

5. Apostrophes

Apostrophes (') are used to combine words into a shorter version of the word (a contraction) or to show possession (ownership).

Using Apostrophes
We use apostrophes for indicating:

1. Possession
If there is one owner: 's (Trabue's office hours)
If there is more than one owner: s' (three instructors' office hours)
If there is more than one owner but the word is already plural: 's (people's study
    habits)

2. Contractions
These are combined words that leave out some of the letters.

A Special Note: It's vs. Its
It's = It is
Its = possession (The syllabus has its own rules.)
We *do not* use apostrophes for plurals not indicating possession.
    College instructor's give students' a lot of homework. (Incorrect)

A. Explanation and Examples
Use an apostrophe in a contraction to represent any missing letters. Use an apostrophe and the letter *s* to make a nouns possessive (show belonging). Do not make the mistake of adding an apostrophe to form the plural of a non-possessive noun. For example, the plural of *book* is *books*, not *book's*.

1. Contractions
Contractions are combined words that leave out some of the letters. The apostrophe in a contraction represents the missing letters, as in the three examples that follow:

1. Isn't (Is not)
2. I'll (I will)
3. They're (They are)

Always include the apostrophe when writing a contraction—it isn't optional.

2. Possessives

Apostrophes can show ownership or belonging. Singular nouns (only one) use an apostrophe with the letter s.

> The instructor's office (Correct)

> The building's entrance (Correct)

This is true even if a singular noun already ends in *s*.

> The gas's odor (Correct)

> The mass's value (Correct)

If a noun is plural (more than one) and ends in *s*, add only the apostrophe.

> The students' residence hall (Correct)

> The teachers' break room (Correct)

Some plural nouns don't end in *s*. In these cases, we follow the standard of an apostrophe with the letter s.

> The people's representative (Correct)

> The women's basketball team (Correct)

Do not use an apostrophe to make a singular word plural.

> The professor's met in the conference room. (Incorrect)

For most regular nouns, you make a plural by adding the letter s to the end of the word.

> The professors met in the conference room. (Correct)

An apostrophe with the letter *s* indicates ownership or a contraction of word. Neither of these work in the following example:

> The student's worked together on their project. (Incorrect)

There is more than one student, so you need to make the subject plural by adding the letter *s*.

> The students worked together on their project. (Correct)

B. Commonly Confused Examples

Certain words that use an apostrophe are easily confused with other words. Be familiar with these examples.

1. It's vs. Its

The word *it* poses a problem, because it can be part of a contraction or a possessive. You'll need to memorize this one and check it every time.

It's = it is

It's a beautiful day. (Correct)

Its = belonging to it

Every strategy has its advantages. (Correct)

2. Your vs. You're

Your is the possessive for the pronoun *you*.

Don't forget your bag. (Correct)

You're is the contraction for *you are*.

You're an excellent note-taker. (Correct)

3. Their, There, They're

Their is possessive for *they*.

The team left for their game. (Correct)

There refers to a place.

I see an available computer station over there. (Correct)

They're is the contraction for *they are*.

They're bringing snacks to the study session. (Correct)

C. More Examples

As you look at each of the incorrect versions below, try to identify what is wrong. Then try to think of a way to fix it. Use the corrected version to help you understand the issue and how to correct it.

Look closely at the following example:

The term has reached it's conclusion. (Incorrect)

The possessive form of *it* doesn't require an apostrophe.

The term has reached **its** conclusion. (Correct)

Can you find the problem in the following example?

Please join you're study group. (Incorrect)

You're means *you are.* The possessive form of *you* is *your.*

Please join **your** study group. (Correct)

D. Practice

Test your understanding by fixing these examples. We've helped you with the first few.

> 1. Be sure to drink plenty of water throughout the day to keep your hydration level at **it's** prime.

(This is the wrong form of the bolded word.)

> 2. Analysis means to examine information and break it down into **it's** parts.

(This is the wrong form of the bolded word.)

> 3. **Its** great to have a sense of direction about what you want to study.

(This is the wrong form of the bolded word.)

> 4. Cognitive **scientist's** will tell you that learning is better accomplished when you use as many ways of representing information as possible.

(Incorrect apostrophe usage in the word *scientists*.)

> 5. Your **professor's** expect you to demonstrate what you learned.

---

6. By giving honest feedback on others' work, you show respect for **they're** process.

_____

7. Being mindful about how you use **you're** time reflects that freedom to choose your life's path.

_____

8. Use your **professors** expectations to guide the kind of feedback to gather and to give during peer review.

_____

9. **Their** on the school basketball team.

_____

10. **Your** more likely to succeed in college if you can focus.

_____

6. Commas

A **comma** (,) is a punctuation mark used to separate items without ending a sentence. Commas are often used incorrectly. Learn the most common rules for commas to make your writing clear.

Commas: Six Common Uses
1. To separate items in a list of three or more (or two, if both are adjectives)
2. Plus FANBOYS to join two complete sentences
3. After introductory phrases
4. Around interrupters/parenthetical phrases
5. Between quotations and their attributions
6. For formatting numbers, dates, titles, addresses or geographic locations

A. Explanation and Examples

Use commas sparingly. If you can't think of a rule for comma usage that applies, you probably don't need one. Occasionally, you may need a comma to clarify the meaning of a sentence, but this is rare. Keep the following rules in mind, and you'll know when to use a comma in almost every situation.

1. Between Items in a List
Use a comma when you are listing more than two things. The list can be objects, actions, or even phrases.

In the following sentence, commas separate nouns in a list.

> College expects you to grow through investigation, trial and error, and correction. (Correct)

Here, commas separate a series of verbs.

> You can recognize, understand, and influence the emotions of others. (Correct)

Commas in this example mark a series of phrases.

> Don't assume your professors will regularly remind you about class assignments, accept late work, or offer extra credit to make up for missed assignments or low scores. (Correct)

2. Between Multiple Adjectives
Adjectives are words that describe nouns (people, places, objects). When more than one adjective describes a noun, separate them with a comma.

> Regardless of how comfortable you feel with anyone on a college campus, maintain a neutral, academic persona in all forms of communication. (Correct)

Don't use a comma between adjectives that always appear in a specific order.

> Students must have three important underlying beliefs in place — a growth mindset, an internal locus of control, and self-efficacy. (Correct)

These adjectives must always go in this order to sound appropriate, so no commas are used. For example, we wouldn't ever write, "important three underlying beliefs."

3. Between Complete Sentences
Place the comma before a coordinating conjunction when joining two complete sentences. Remember FANBOYS to recall the coordinating conjunctions: *for, and, nor, but, or, yet, so.*

To review complete sentences, see "Run-Ons" in Part 3, Section 2.

> Your persona at home might be different than your persona at school, but the knowledge you've gained outside of school can help you to develop an effective persona as a college student. (Correct)

Comma + *but* join two complete sentences here.

4. After Introductory Phrases

Place a comma after any introductory phrases that appear before the main part of the sentence.

> As you navigate through college, you should present yourself in a way that meets the expectations of the college culture. (Correct)

5. Around Parenthetical Phrases

If a phrase adds optional details after a word, surround that parenthetical phrase with commas.

> Some courses, such as anatomy and physiology, may require even more time. (Correct)

> Stephen Covey, a well-known author and educator, spent much of his career teaching people how to be positive and successful. (Correct)

However, if the phrase is necessary to the meaning of the sentence, don't use the commas.

> The courses anatomy and physiology may require even more time. (Correct)

> Well-known author and educator Stephen Covey spent much of his career teaching people how to be positive and successful. (Correct)

6. Between Attribution and a Quotation

Place a comma after the words that introduce a direct quotation.

> Henry Ford said, "Whether you believe you can do a thing or not, you are right." (Correct)

No comma is needed when the quotation is preceded by the word *that*.

> Henry Ford said that "Whether you believe you can do a thing or not, you are right." (Correct)

7. For Formatting Numbers, Dates, and Titles

Use commas when writing numerals longer than three digits, dates that include the year, and names with suffixes (such as Jr. or Sr.).

> 1,000,000 (Correct)

> January 1, 1983 (Correct)

> Henry Louis Gates, Jr. (Correct)

8. Do not place a single comma between a subject and its verb.

Even if a sentence is long, the subject and verb should not be separated by one comma.

> Students who schedule their time carefully, are more likely to complete assignments. (Incorrect)

The sentence should not have a comma. The subject *student* goes with the verb *are*.

> Students who schedule their time carefully are more likely to complete assignments. (Correct)

B. More Examples

As you look at each of the incorrect versions below, try to identify what is wrong. Then try to think of a way to fix it. Use the corrected version to help you understand the issue and how to correct it.

Take a look at the following example. Do you see where the introductory phrase ends and the main idea begins?

> After next term I'll be done with my math classes. (Incorrect)

To fix, use a comma to separate the introductory phrase from the rest of the sentence.

> After next term, I'll be done with my math classes. (Correct)

Adding a comma does not always solve the problem, as in the following example:

> Books in the reference section, must stay in the library. (Incorrect)

To fix, remove the comma. Remember, a single comma should not appear between the subject and its verb.

> Books in the reference section must stay in the library. (Correct)

C. Practice
Test your understanding by fixing these examples. We've helped you with the first few.

1. Long-term goals are great but it's also important to have short-term goals.

(This example has two complete sentences. Separate them using one of the standard methods.)

2. However not all external rewards are actually all that healthy for you over the long term.

(Use a comma after introductory words.)

3. When the external motivation comes in the form of pleasing people the motivation usually weakens as you move forward in your life.

(Use a comma after introductory phrases.)

4. Three powerful sources of internal motivation are autonomy mastery and purpose.

(Separate items in a list with commas.)

5. Whenever you get better at something you value your motivation to work harder and longer increases.

6. Vonnegut says "We are what we imagine ourselves to be."

---

7. Napoleon Hill stated that, "Goals are dreams with a deadline."

---

8. William Glasser a renowned psychiatrist and educational theorist developed a treatment approach called "reality therapy."

---

9. Oprah Winfrey the famous talk-show host said that "the greatest lesson of life is that you are responsible for your own life."

---

10. *Brown vs. Board of Education* ended segregated education on September 2 1958.

---

11. Bloom's Taxonomy named for educational psychologist Benjamin Bloom identifies six different types of academic questions or thinking tasks.

---

7. Capitalization

Use **capitalization** (a large first letter) to mark significant words. The rules of capitalization relate to sentence position, proper nouns, and titles.

A. Explanation and Examples

Follow standard rules for uppercase letters. Always capitalize the following:

1. First Letter of Sentences
Capitalize the first letter of every sentence.

> College is more than the sum of its classrooms. (Correct)

2. First Letter of Proper Nouns
Proper nouns are the name of people, places, brands, and titles.

> Commencement began with an address from President Howard. (Correct)

> Traffic backed up near the school on Lancaster Drive. (Correct)

Here's an important tip to remember: English capitalizes the months of the year, but it doesn't capitalize the seasons. For example, "In September, summer turns into fall."

3. First Letter in Quoted Text
Capitalize the first letter of a quotation.

> Winston Churchill said, "Success is not final." (Correct)

Do not capitalize the first letter if a quotation continues after an attribution that interrupts.

> "Please," said the teacher, "sit down wherever you like." (Correct)

4. First Letters of Major Words in Titles

Capitalize all of the words in the title of a published work, except articles, prepositions, and conjunctions.

1. Articles = *a, an, the*
2. Prepositions = words that show relationships (examples: *in, on, under, around, through, for*)
3. Conjunctions = words that join (FANBOYS—*for, and, nor, but, or, yet, so*); words that introduce a phrase (examples: *although, while, as, because*)

> My writing class uses the textbook entitled *The Structure of Argument.* (Correct)

> George Elliot wrote the novel *The Mill on the Floss.* (Correct)

5. The Pronoun I

Capitalize all forms of the pronoun I.

> When I go to practice, I get a good workout. (Correct)

> After the exam, I'm going to take a nap. (Correct)

A word processor should catch most capitalization errors, but it's still your responsibility to know these rules and review your work.

B. More Examples

As you look at each of the incorrect versions below, try to identify what is wrong. Then try to think of a way to fix it. Use the corrected version to help you understand the issue and how to correct it.

In the following example, which words should be capitalized?

> When i transfer, i plan to study veterinary medicine. (Incorrect)

The pronoun I is always capitalized.

> When I transfer, I plan to study veterinary medicine. (Correct)

In the following example, which words should be capitalized?

> My instructor recommended the book deep work by Cal Newport. (Incorrect)

The first letter of major words in titles are capitalized.

> My instructor recommended the book *Deep Work* by Cal Newport. (Correct)

C. Practice

Test your understanding by fixing these examples. We've helped you with the first few.

1. value the time you have.

(Capitalize the first word in sentences.)

_____

2. your ideas are not you.

(Capitalize the first word in sentences.)

_____

3. Arthur l. costa proposed a framework to organize types of thinking.

(Capitalize the first letter of last names.)

_____

4. The cornell note-taking system from cornell university is one popular and easy method.
(Capitalize the first letter of proper nouns.)

_____

5. Carl jung says, "we cannot change anything unless we accept it."

_____

6. Watch the video "how to make stress your friend" by kelly mcGonigal.

_____

7. The *new york times* published the article "what google learned from its quest to build the perfect team," by charles duhigg.

_____

8. When i registered, i checked the prerequisites for the class.

_____

9. i bought a copy of *make college yours* at the bookstore.

_____

10. Be careful when using google to find sources.

_____

8. Spelling

Spelling can be one of the most difficult parts of writing to master. It remains important, however, in showing the reader your exact meaning.

A. Explanation and Examples

Technology makes it easy to check spelling. Ultimately, however, it's still your responsibility to keep your writing free from spelling issues.

1. Use Spell-Check

If you write using a word processor, confirm that the spell-check is turned on and is working. Look for a wavy red line under words that are misspelled. If you right-click on the underlined word, your word processor may offer suggestions for the word you meant. If you click on one of these, be sure it's the correct word.

2. Commonly Confused Words

Pay attention to sets of words that are often mistaken for each other. A spell-checker on your device won't necessarily catch these commonly confused words. If you are aware of these sets, you can confirm that you've written the correct word when you edit. Take a look at the following examples:

Your Guide to College Writing (Chemeketa Press 2021) reviews many commonly confused words in the chapter on Word Choice (the list begins on page 146).

1. Accept/except
2. Advice/advise
3. Affect/effect
4. All ready/already
5. Bare/bear
6. Breath/breathe
7. Cite/site
8. Illusion/allusion
9. Principal/principle
10. Red/read
11. Straight/strait
12. Than/then
13. There/their/they're
14. To/too/two
15. Whether/weather/wether

Sometimes, a word processor will indicate when you're using the wrong one of these, but not always. Learn the difference between these confusing sets of words so you can spot them yourself.

B. More Examples

As you look at each of the incorrect versions below, try to identify what is wrong. Then try to think of a way to fix it. Use the corrected version to help you understand the issue and how to correct it.

Read carefully to find the misused word in the following example:

> I'm required to site my sources in the research paper. (Incorrect)

Site refers to a location. Cite means to mention a source.

> I'm required to cite my sources in the research paper. (Correct)

See if you can spot another commonly confused word in the following example:

> Students can visit Career Services for job advise. (Incorrect)

Advise is a verb meaning "to offer recommendations." Advice is a noun for the recommendations themselves.

> Students can visit Career Services for job advice. (Correct)

C. Practice

Test your understanding by fixing these examples. We've helped you with the first few.

1. Social awareness is the ability **too** know or gauge how **too** behave in different social situations and environments.

(The replace the bolded term with the correct word.)

_____

2. Students **bare** some responsibility for a safe classroom.

(The replace the bolded term with the correct word.)

_____

3. Your college persona has to respond to a classroom activity by **excepting** it as another opportunity to investigate new ideas and make them your own.

(The replace the bolded term with the correct word.)

_____

4. Personal agency is the belief that you can control and **effect** the outcome of many of the situations you face.

(The replace the bolded term with the correct word.)

_____

5. If you haven't **all ready** done so, identify and develop a network that supports you.

_____

6. Libraries often have staff on **cite** to help students use computer applications.

___

7. Be **straitforward** with yourself and your professor about any mistakes you make.

___

8. A practical exam involves a student physically demonstrating **there** knowledge of a skill.

___

9. Procrastination is putting an assignment or other task off longer **then** you should.

___

10. Academic integrity calls for you to be the best version of yourself as a learner, regardless of **weather** or not other people notice.

___

9. Parallelism

Parallelism means keeping a series of words or phrases in the same format. This similarity helps readers to see the connection and better understand what you are saying. Using parallelism also sounds good and adds style.

A. Explanation and Examples

When a sentence has a series of words or phrases, keep those words or phrases similar to make them parallel.

1. Words

Parallelism can be seen in the repetition of words ending in *-ing* in the following example.

> I enjoy walking, meditating, and cooking. (Correct)

Observe the difference when the same sentence lacks parallelism. Not only is the following example grammatically incorrect, but it is also harder to read because the corresponding parts are not balanced.

> I enjoy walking, meditating, and I like to cook. (Incorrect)

Sometimes, a pair of parallel words are simply joined with a coordinating conjunction (FANBOYS).

> Students should rest and exercise. (Correct)

However, verbs in the same sentence should be in the same form. The following example incorrectly pairs a regular verb (*rest*) with an infinitive (*to exercise*).

> Students should rest and to exercise. (Incorrect)

When you have more than two parallel words, you can link them with commas and a coordinating conjunction before the final word.

> Students should rest, exercise, and eat properly. (Correct)

2. Phrases

Parallelism applies to lists of words, but it also applies to entire phrases.

Notice how the following phrases are similar in this example:

> My instructor said that I needed to revise my thesis, improve my transitions, and proofread my essay. (Correct)

Again, this would not work as well if the phrases were not parallel, as in the following example:

> My instructor said that I needed to revise my thesis, my transitions were bad, and could I please do a better job of proofreading? (Incorrect)

Phrases that tend to go in parallel lists include these types of words:

1. **Infinitives**—verbs that go with the word *to*; for example, *to say, to walk, to think*.
2. **Gerunds**—nouns formed from verbs ending in *-ing*; for example, *reading, writing,* and *computing*.

B. More Examples

As you look at each of the incorrect versions below, try to identify what is wrong. Then try to think of a way to fix it. Use the corrected version to help you understand the issue and how to correct it.

The following sentence is not parallel. Can you find where the parallelism breaks down?

> Students who participate well are attentive, thoughtful, and they show respect. (Incorrect)

The following sentence uses parallel adjectives to describe the ideal student:

> Students who participate well are attentive, thoughtful, and respectful. (Correct)

It can sometimes be challenging to keep longer sentences parallel, as in this example:

> The essay argued that sleep sharpened memory, that it improved mood, and made the immune system stronger. (Incorrect)

To fix the problem, this sentence needs parallel phrases that describes the essay's argument:

> The essay argued that sleep sharpened memory, improved mood, and strengthened the immune system. (Correct)

C. Practice

Test your understanding by fixing these examples. We've helped you with the first few.

1. You're responsible for **knowing** and **to meet** application deadlines for financial aid.

(Make the bolded terms parallel by rewriting as necessary.)

2. **Synthesize** means to gather information, understand it, analyze it, combine it with your prior knowledge and **developing** a new concept or creation with it.

(Make the bolded terms parallel by rewriting as necessary.)

3. During a peer review, students offer feedback, help each other, and **giving** praise.

(Make the bolded terms parallel by rewriting as necessary.)

4. Mapping is a note-taking method that helps students with organizing, analyzing, and **to encode** information.

(Make the bolded terms parallel by rewriting as necessary.)

5. People with imposter syndrome compare themselves to others and **are deciding** they do not fit in.

6. A college persona is learning-focused, collaborative, and **it respects**.

_____

7. Use a variety of thinking strategies such as recalling, paraphrasing, questioning, classifying, comparing, and **to contrast** content.

_____

8. A greater number of credits means more class lectures, more assignments, and **deadlines**.

_____

9. Successful students know it is important to study hard, to be organized, and **being in communication** with instructors.

_____

10. An excellent professor is smart, understandable, and **they are easy to approach**.

_____

10. Word Choice

Your **word choice** impacts your reader. Be careful to use words that mean exactly what you think they do. Your word use should be both specific and accurate, as explained below.

A. Explanation and Examples

1. Specific

Word choice must be specific. This means choosing words that mean something particular, rather than something general. It's easy to think of a word that could fit into many sentences, but this type of word usually doesn't tell the reader exactly what you mean.

Look at the use of the words *author* and *stuff* in the example below. The words in this sentence don't offer enough information. Who is the author? What exactly did the author say?

> The author said stuff. (Poor)

Now let's look at a sentence that is more specific. This version specifically states who the author was and what they stated.

> Stephen King says that horror movies help people. (Better)

The sentence above includes the word *says*. While there's nothing wrong with *says*, a more specific word would be helpful.

> Stephen King argues that horror movies provide a kind of mental relief. (Even better)

Argues offers a more specific verb to describe the author's communication. Now the reader has a sense of Stephen King's goal, as well as how this writer is interpreting Stephen King. This version also explains King's thesis in greater detail.

2. Accurate

Word choice must be also be accurate. This means that you should check that a word means what you think it does. Sometimes, students use a word because it sounds impressive, but they use it incorrectly.

The following example uses the word *defiantly*, which means making a big show of going against something or someone. This is the wrong word. The author means *definitely*.

I defiantly agree with the author's thesis. (Incorrect)

Here, *definitely* means to be sure and certain of something.

I definitely agree with the author's thesis. (Correct)

Many students use a thesaurus (a book with lists of similar words). Be mindful that while a thesaurus can help you discover new words, you need to understand the exact meaning of the word before using it. Don't use a word if you're unsure of its specific meaning.

B. More Examples

As you look at each of the incorrect versions below, try to identify what is wrong. Then try to think of a way to fix it. Use the corrected version to help you understand the issue and how to correct it.

The word *he* is non-specific and unclear. Does it refer to the speaker or to Mr. Wilson?

> The speaker and his colleague Mr. Wilson described the historic event. He completely changed my opinion. (Incorrect)

Using a more specific word will make the meaning clear.

> The speaker and his colleague Mr. Wilson described the historic event. The speaker completely changed my opinion. (Correct)

Better yet, the writer could use the names of both people who are describing the event to be even more clear.

In the following example, see if you can find the word that is used incorrectly.

> When I'm stressed, I sometimes need to just take a breathe. (Incorrect)

This is a common mistake. *Breathe* is the verb. *Breath* is the noun.

> When I'm stressed, I sometimes need to just take a breath. (Correct)

For more on commonly confused words, see "Spelling" in Part 3, Section 8.

C. Practice

Test your understanding by fixing these examples. We've helped you with the first few.

1. The lecturer **said** that discrimination was harmful to communities.

(*Said* is generic. Pick more specific word that could fit in this context.)

_____

2. There are **lots of reasons** to go to college.

(List some specific reasons for going to college. Going to college is beneficial because…)

_____

3. Plagiarism is **bad** for a student's academic record.

(This is not specific enough. Use more exact words for why plagiarism is bad. Plagiarism is the act of not giving credit to sources.)

_____

4. The instructor assigned a **very long** essay.

(How many words or pages is very long? Fix this to state a specific length.)

_____

5. The article we read for class was **awesome!**

(Why was it awesome? Use specific words to explain why a source might be particularly good.)

_____

6. The student **inferred** that she had been absent because of health problems.

(This is the wrong use of the word *inferred*. Use a dictionary if needed to identify the correct use of the word.)

7. The committee was not **adverse** to proposal.

(Use a dictionary if needed to identify the correct use of the word.)

8. **Except** that rewards are worth the effort.

(This is the wrong use of the word *except*. Use a dictionary if needed to identify a correct word for the sentence.)

9. Jot down important facts, ideas, **principals**, or memory cues to help you with an exam.

(The word *principal* refers to the person in charge of a school. It's commonly confused with a similar word. Use a dictionary if needed to identify the correct word for the sentence.)

10. Take time to write down everything that you have to do in a place that you will look at **everyday**.

(*Everyday* means "ordinary," as in "these are my everyday chores." Fix this to mean that something happens once per day.)

Part 4

Appendix

Revision Exercise 1

Student Sample: Personal Narrative

For the following revision exercise (figure A.1), read through the essay and note the numbered highlighting of certain parts of the text. Here's the prompt for the personal narrative essay:

> Tell the story of a time at school or college where you succeeded (or failed) at an academic moment. This is the story of a time when a strategy you employed as a student went well, or went wrong, and incorporates lots of rich detail about that time. What was the context or background? What happened? What were the reasons behind the success or failure? Looking back, what did you learn from that experience?

The highlighted passages indicate common structure, organization, and content issues. Match each highlighted section with its mention in the box at the bottom of the essay.

Annotations

A. This introduction could use more detail. Add background and context to the information to follow.
B. This conclusion has more than one central idea. Provide a suggestion to help the author make the last paragraph more cohesive.
C. This sentence doesn't match the rest of the essay because it is about the future. Revise it to better reflect the main ideas of the essay and the assignment prompt.
D. This description is unique but distracting in this context. Change this sentence to explain the surprise in a more appropriate way.
E. This title reflects the assignment rather than the content. Provide an alternate title.
F. This information does not support the ideas expressed in the essay and can be removed in the revision process. Suggest a way to rephrase or cut.
G. This paragraph is important because it shows the moment the author realizes what needs to change; however, it is lacking in details. Provide supporting information to illustrate the idea here.

Figure A.1a. Student Essay Sample. Page 1.

Student Name

Instructor Name

WR090

April 16, 2019

Essay 1

To say I've had my fair share of academic challenges in school would be an understatement, but there is a particular time where that failure finally took its toll on me. After that failure, I decided to take a step back, breathe, give myself time, and finally went back in with a mindset I had not had before. I hope to remain as successful as I have been with this new mindset and I hope this new mindset is consistent and here to stay.

When I was 21, I decided to go to college. I wasn't sure what exactly I wanted my field of study to be, but I felt as though it was almost a sort of "task" that needed to be accomplished. At the time, I was working part-time retail jobs and wasn't headed towards a specific direction. When I had signed up for courses, I aimed towards courses that interested me rather than courses that would benefit me in the future.

Not only did I have no sense of direction, but I also had absolutely no organizational skills. I remember walking into Chemeketa with my sister and

Answer: _____

Explanation: _____

_____

_____

_____

_____

_____

Answer: _____

Explanation: _____

_____

_____

_____

_____

_____

Answer: _____

Explanation: _____

_____

_____

_____

_____

_____

Nice work! This topic sentence transitions from the main idea of the last paragraph (lacking direction) and ties it to the main idea of this paragraph (organization skills).

Figure A.1b. Student Essay Sample. Page 2.

thinking "I should sign up too." I was already a week late into the term and did not take into consideration the amount of work it would take to catch up. Aside from a different schedule, I went into college thinking it wouldn't be a drastic change from high school and I was sure I didn't miss much that first week. With no clue on what I was doing, I proceeded to register.

I was soon to learn a big lesson: just because you have the liberty of choosing if you want to show up to your 8:30 am class does not mean that you should miss that class. Since I didn't have a car at the time, my only form of transportation was the bus. This means instead of leaving my house 10 minutes early, I would need to leave at least an hour early to make it on time and I did not realize I wasn't ready for that kind of commitment. I know what you're thinking, and I agree. I also want to shake my past self and yell, "WHAT ARE YOU DOING?!" It's almost like watching a scary movie, except I wasn't aware I was the lead role who was continuously making these terrible unconscious decisions.

Although I managed to make it to class for the most part – except for that 8:30 am class of course – I couldn't seem to grasp the concept of time and how essential deadlines are. I would sit in class and listen to everything

Good start! Adding a key term such as "organization" or "planning" could help expand this example.

Figure A.1c. Student Essay Sample. Page 3.

my instructor had to say, but it was a rare occasion when I would note down assignments that were due. I would tell myself that I would remember what the assignment was, but when the deadline was near, I couldn't remember the exact instructions. On the seldom occasion that I would note down the due date, I couldn't be bothered to look at my planner. I found lounging around and snacking all day long as a better use of my time. I would start a big project and would find myself hanging out with friends not even halfway through. Anything was better than having to do homework.

Needless to say, I did not do well. I came out with hardly any credits and those credits were only because I took P.E classes and you would need to put some good effort in to fail a P.E. class. The sad thing is this wasn't my last failure. This was just the beginning of my college failure. I went through a couple terms going through this same failure with the exact same issues each time. After about my fourth attempt, I finally realized what I was doing and how I was only hindering myself throughout this process. I realized that going to school without a goal was not a good step for me. That's when I decided going to school was not meant to be for the time being and I ended up taking a long break.

Figure A.1d. Student Essay Sample. Page 4.

Answer: _____

Explanation:_____

_____

_____

_____

_____

_____

_____

_____

Answer: _____

Explanation:_____

_____

_____

_____

_____

_____

_____

_____

Name   4

Summer of 2016 came, and I was now 23. I was completely content with where I was in life and had no intentions of going back to school. Suddenly, it hit me like a sock full of refrigerated butter. I wanted to become a nurse or something similar to it. It all seemed so obvious I couldn't help but think how I hadn't figured this out before. I had always wanted to try medical assisting, but never stopped to think of it as an actual career.

This time felt different. This time I felt like a whole new me that I had never met before. I walked into the college knowing exactly what my intentions were. I had even done research before going to a counselor and knew which classes I needed to take to accomplish this newfound goal. I had been meeting with this counselor since I had started at Chemeketa and she could see there was something different about this time. We spent some time reminiscing about my past failures and had a few laughs about them.

Although I was much older than before and had matured quite a bit since then, I now had new obstacles I would need to overcome. I was now married, a mother to an eight-month-old daughter, working part-time, and struggling heavily with exhaustion. With these new (and a lot more trying) obstacles, I knew I had to do everything differently. I had to put a lot more effort in than ever before. Doing absolutely nothing was no longer an option.

Figure A.1e. Student Essay Sample. Page 5.

Name   5

I knew that getting into the Medical Assisting program would be competitive and someone who can't pass a class is not at the top of their priority list. Now that I had a lot more responsibilities outside of school, I decided to go through with online school. This created another obstacle as online courses require a lot more self-discipline.

The first day of the term I sat myself down, printed out every single syllabus, separated every class by folder, and wrote due dates down on a planner and a work calendar. From there, I would spend as much of my free time doing homework and would go as far as doing school assignments during work hours (don't tell my boss). This proved to be extremely efficient as I was able to pass with a B average.

This experience proved to me that the issue was not that school wasn't meant for me. The issue was that I was not motivated or determined. There was no end goal. Now that I have a vision for myself, everything has changed. Although I am making up for failed courses and I am now taking more courses than the previous term, I know that I can overcome these obstacles, no matter how challenging, as long as I stick with this new routine.

Answer: _____

Explanation: _____

_____

_____

_____

_____

_____

_____

_____

Answer: _____

Explanation: _____

_____

_____

_____

_____

_____

_____

_____

_____

_____

Proofreading Exercise 1

Student Sample: Personal Narrative

For the following proofreading exercise (figure A.2), read through the essay and note the numbered highlighting of certain parts of the text. Here's the prompt for the personal narrative essay:

> Tell the story of a time at school or college where you succeeded (or failed) at an academic moment. This is the story of a time when a strategy you employed as a student went well, or went wrong, and incorporates lots of rich detail about that time. What was the context or background? What happened? What were the reasons behind the success or failure? Looking back, what did you learn from that experience?

The highlighted passages indicate common grammar, punctuation, sentence boundary, and academic word choice issues. Match each highlighted section with its mention in the box at the bottom of the essay.

Annotations

A. This sentence has introductory words. Add a comma in the correct place.
B. This sentence needs punctuation at the end. Add the missing punctuation mark.
C. This sentence needs punctuation between introductory words and a quotation. Place the missing punctuation mark in the correct place.
D. The same word is repeated twice in this sentence. Think of a substitute for one of the repeated words.
E. While unique, the description in this sentence is distracting. Rewrite this sentence to explain the surprise in a more appropriate way.
F. This sentence has verbs in more than one tense. Change the verb that doesn't match.
G. This passage is a run-on sentence. Add the missing punctuation mark to fix the run-on.

Figure A.2a. Student Essay Sample. Page 1.

Name   1

Student Name

Instructor's Name

WR090

April 16, 2019

Mission No Longer Impossible

To say I've had my fair share of academic challenges in school would be an understatement, but there is a particular time where that failure finally took its toll on me. I repeatedly struggled through college classes I was not interested in, with no cohesive plan for my future. I started and stopped college three separate times. After that failure, I decided to take a step back, breathe, give myself time, and finally went back in with a mindset I had not had before. I hope to remain as successful as I have been with this new mindset and I hope this new mindset is consistent and here to stay.

When I was 21, I decided to go to college. I wasn't sure what exactly I wanted my field of study to be, but I felt as though it was almost a sort of "task" that needed to be accomplished. At the time, I was working part-time retail jobs and wasn't headed towards a specific direction. When I had signed up for courses, I aimed towards courses that interested me rather than courses that would benefit me in the future.

Answer: _____

Explanation: _____

_____

_____

_____

_____

_____

_____

_____

Figure A.2b. Student Essay Sample. Page 2.

Answer: _____

Explanation: _____

_____

_____

_____

_____

_____

_____

_____

Answer: _____

Explanation: _____

_____

_____

_____

_____

_____

_____

_____

Name   2

Not only did I have no sense of direction, but I also had absolutely no organizational skills. I remember walking into Chemeketa with my sister and thinking "I should sign up too." I was already a week late into the term and did not take into consideration the amount of work it would take to catch up. Aside from a different schedule, I went into college thinking it wouldn't be a drastic change from high school and I was sure I didn't miss much that first week. With no clue on what I was doing, I proceeded to register.

I was soon to learn a big lesson: just because you have the liberty of choosing if you want to show up to your 8:30 a.m. class does not mean that you should miss that class. Since I didn't have a car at the time, my only form of transportation was the bus. This means instead of leaving my house 10 minutes early, I would need to leave at least an hour early to make it on time and I did not realize I wasn't ready for that kind of commitment. I know what you're thinking, and I agree. I also want to shake my past self and yell, "What are you doing?!" It's almost like watching a scary movie, except I wasn't aware I was the lead role who was continuously making these terrible unconscious decisions.

Although I managed to make it to class for the most part – except for that 8:30 a.m. class of course – I couldn't seem to grasp the concept of time

Nice. A comma separates this quotation from the rest of the sentence. The beginning of the quotation is also capitalized correctly.

Figure A.2c. Student Essay Sample. Page 3.

Name   3

and how essential deadlines are. I would sit in class and listen to everything

my instructor had to say, but it was a rare occasion when I would note down

assignments that were due. I would tell myself that I would remember what

the assignment was, but when the deadline was near, I couldn't remember the

exact instructions. On the seldom occasion that I would note down the due

date, I couldn't be bothered to look at my planner. I found lounging around

and snacking all day long as a better use of my time. I would start a big

project and would find myself hanging out with friends not even halfway

through. Anything was better than having to do homework.

Needless to say, I did not do well. I came out with hardly any credits

and those credits were only because I took P.E classes and you would need to

put some good effort in to fail a P.E. class. The sad thing is this wasn't my

last failure. This was just the beginning of my college failure. I went through

a couple terms going through this same failure with the exact same issues

each time. After about my fourth attempt, I finally realized what I was doing

and how I was only hindering myself throughout this process. I realized that

going to school without a goal was not a good step for me. That's when I

decided going to school was not meant to be for the time being and I ended

up taking a long break.

Answer: _____

Explanation: _____

_____

_____

_____

_____

_____

_____

_____

Figure A.2d. Student Essay Sample. Page 4.

Answer: _____

Explanation: _____

_____

_____

_____

_____

_____

_____

_____

*Well done! Less
common words can be
difficult to spell.*

Answer: _____

Explanation: _____

_____

_____

_____

_____

_____

_____

_____

Name   4

Summer of 2016 came, and I was now 23. I was completely content with where I was in life and had no intentions of going back to school. Suddenly, it hit me like a sock full of refrigerated butter. I wanted to become a nurse or something similar to it. It all seemed so obvious I couldn't help but think how I hadn't figured this out before. I had always wanted to try medical assisting, but never stopped to think of it as an actual career. With that being said, I decided to go back to school.

This time felt different. This time I felt like a whole new me that I had never met before. I walked into the college knowing exactly what my intentions were. I had even done research before going to a counselor and knew which classes I needed to take to accomplish this newfound goal. I had been meeting with this counselor since I had started at Chemeketa and he could see there was something different about this time. We spent some time reminiscing about my past failures and had a few laughs about them.

Although I was much older than before and had matured quite a bit since then, I now had new obstacles I would need to overcome. I was now married, a mother to an eight-month-old daughter, working part-time, and struggling with exhaustion. With these new (and a lot more trying) obstacles, I knew I have to do everything differently. I had to put a lot more effort in

Figure A.2e. Student Essay Sample. Page 5.

than ever before. Doing absolutely nothing was no longer an option. I knew that getting into the Medical Assisting program would be competitive and someone who can't pass a class is not at the top of their priority list. Now that I had a lot more responsibilities outside of school, I decided to go through with online school. This created another obstacle as online courses require a lot more self-discipline.

The first day of the term I sat myself down, printed out every single syllabus, separated every class by folder, and wrote due dates down on a planner and a work calendar. From there, I would spend as much of my free time doing homework and I would go as far as doing school assignments during work hours. This proved to be extremely efficient as I was able to pass with a B average.

This experience proved to me that the issue was not that school wasn't meant for me. The issue was that I was not motivated or determined. There was no end goal. Now that I have a vision for myself, everything has changed. Although I am making up for failed courses and I am now taking more courses than the previous term, I know that I can overcome these obstacles, no matter how challenging, as long as I stick with this new routine

Answer: _____

Explanation: _____

_____

_____

_____

_____

_____

_____

_____

Revision Exercise 2

Student Sample: Expository Essay

For the following revision exercise (figure A.3), read through the essay and note the numbered highlighting of certain parts of the text. Here's the prompt for the expository essay:

> Your essay will introduce an academic issue or problem (here, the student chose work/life balance issues while in college) that a student can encounter at college and take a position on what might help a student overcome it, investigate aspect(s) of what makes a student successful at college in relation to the problem, and conclude with an evaluation or recommendation based on the research and personal experience you include in your paper. If helpful, think beyond the single student, to systems and administration—the way college works—to identify the potential source (or possible solution) of/to an issue. You might also consider the context—why is this issue important? To complete this essay, you will incorporate at least one outside resource into your essay.

The highlighted passages indicate common structure, organization, and content issues. Match each highlighted section with its mention in the box at the bottom of the essay.

Annotations

A. This passage offers the definition of a common word. Consider a more unique piece of information the student might include here instead.

B. This essay lacks a title. Suggest a title that helps the reader understand what the essay is about.

C. This quotation needs introduction and explanation. Add information about the source before the quotation and explanation about the significance of the source.

D. This conclusion doesn't remind the reader of the essay's key points. What more could be added here?

E. The introduction to this paragraph mentions "second place" without stating what is in "first place." How could this sentence be revised to clarify the idea here?

F. This thesis statement is a good start, but it needs to fit the scope of the essay. How could you modify this sentence to create more clarity for the reader of what's to come?

G. This paragraph uses a quotation or paraphrase instead of a topic sentence. Locate this spot, and indicate where you might relocate it within its paragraph.

Figure A.3a. Student Essay Sample. Page 1.

Name   1

Student Name

Instructor Name

Course Name

Due Date

"Warning! Challenges ahead!" would be a great motto for individuals who embark on the journey of juggling work, life, school, and obligations while in college. A majority of college students who work and attend school find balance to be a real struggle. Life is naturally challenging; balancing work and school while also attempting to meet other demands that scream for attention can easily become overwhelming. There can be many obstacles to navigate in all aspects of life, and college is not an exception. Students who work while attending college have increased stress because it's an additional layer of responsibility. It's important that students manage their time well.

When I start to feel overwhelmed and pulled in too many directions, I stop and prioritize my health. I have a constant list of things that need to be accomplished and that list gets prioritized as well. These little tasks don't sound like much, but compounded on top of all the other obligations and responsibilities, it makes the balancing act more difficult and time consuming. It's important to

Answer: _____

Explanation:_____

_____

_____

_____

_____

_____

_____

_____

Answer: _____

Explanation:_____

_____

_____

_____

_____

_____

_____

_____

_____

Figure A.3b. Student Essay Sample. Page 2.

Answer: _____

Explanation: _____

_____

_____

_____

_____

_____

_____

_____

Answer: _____

Explanation: _____

_____

_____

_____

_____

_____

_____

_____

Name   2

trust in my own ability and believe I have what it takes to successfully manage

and balance work, school, and life demands. I suggest to anyone who is working

while attending school, to keep your family posted and up to date on what's going

on. My family's support and encouragement is a tremendous help. It allows me

the capacity to focus on school, making it a commensurate priority to work.

    Managing multiple responsibilities is a real stressor that can lead to burnout.

Oxford languages defines "burnout" as "To ruin one's health or become

completely exhausted through overwork." Students should prioritize self care and

incorporate healthy boundaries and habits to reduce stress. "For some students,

working full-time may even be a necessity which can lead to a neglect of self

care"(Estrada 2). Estrada speaks with former academic advisor Jennifer

Wonderly, who discusses the signs of overworking: "Missing class is a huge one,

and sometimes they're missing class due to work or just from oversleeping

because they are physically exhausted," said Wonderly, "My experience in

academic advising is that when students go on academic probation, it's usually not

because of not having the academic ability, it's usually due to time management

issues and competing obligations" (qtd. in Estrada 2). When work is absolutely

essential to meeting basic needs, this ranks the priority, and automatically

appoints work as a greater importance and school by default is secondary to that.

Figure A.3c. Student Essay Sample. Page 3.

Name   3

Megan Sovona, a current college student working full time claims, "Time

becomes even more valuable when balancing work, life and school. Sadly I don't

have the option to work less, if anything I find myself needing to work more just

to cover all the bills. Finding extra time to relax and unwind is challenging.

Something always needs to get done and the never ending "to do" list can be

exhausting." Sovona stresses the significance of having good communication and

support from her college academic advisors and to be aware of the programs

colleges offer. "Take advantage of the programs offered, they can be a huge asset

in helping you achieve your goals and overcome obstacles. Don't be afraid to ask

for help," says Sovona. Time is a finite resource for working students.

Pursuing a degree that is in second place on the priority list is a significant

challenge in itself. I try to give each responsibility equal priority, but I work part

time as a CAN while pursuing a degree. Working is non negotiable. I have a

mortgage, I have a partner, I have commitments and obligations. Balancing all of

this is stressful, especially when work conflicts with school obligations. My

experience has also shown me that proper planning and time management, as well

as keeping your employer well informed and expressing your needs, can lessen

the impact work will have on school life. For me, time management plays a

remarkable role in how things balance out. Everything must be scheduled and

Well done! Mentioning the source in an introductory phrase is an effective way to include a quotation.

Answer: _____

Explanation: _____

_____

_____

_____

_____

_____

_____

_____

_____

Figure A.3d. Student Essay Sample. Page 4.

Answer: _____

Explanation: _____

_____

_____

_____

_____

_____

_____

Name   4

prioritized. I have to be purposeful in how I spend my time. If I have scheduled a

block of time to work on a paper, I have to be unwilling to surrender that priority

in order to spend time my family.

    According to MHA, Mental Health America's website, "Feeling overloaded

can seriously damage your mind and body, making you more vulnerable to

physical and mental health problems. Additionally, chronic stress keeps you from

being your best self. While stress is not inherently bad, it's important to find

healthy ways to deal with it" ("Balancing Work and School"). For many students,

working is a necessity while attending college. It is a struggle that adds stressors

in their lives. Time becomes such a valuable commodity that self neglect often

occurs. To avoid fewer bumps in the road, it is crucial to make self care a priority

to avoid burnout. Something I do to help avoid burnout is to make sure I have one

day a week that is completely free from work and school responsibilities. I do

have to plan properly and make sure the majority of course and study work is

completed to achieve this.

    When students are struggling to make ends meet, it is important that they

educate themselves. Working students should also communicate and express their

needs to employers.

Nice! This passage follows the assignment instructions by offering a recommendation based on personal experience.

Answer: _____

Explanation: _____

_____

_____

Proofreading Exercise 2

Student Sample: Expository Essay

For the following proofreading exercise (figure A.4), read through the essay and note the numbered highlighting of certain parts of the text. Here's the prompt for the expository essay:

> Your essay will introduce an academic issue or problem (here, the student chose work/life balance issues while in college) that a student can encounter at college and take a position on what might help a student overcome it, investigate aspect(s) of what makes a student successful at college in relation to the problem, and conclude with an evaluation or recommendation based on the research and personal experience you include in your paper. If helpful, think beyond the single student, to systems and administration—the way college works—to identify the potential source (or possible solution) of/to an issue. You might also consider the context—why is this issue important? To complete this essay, you will incorporate at least one outside resource into your essay.

The highlighted passages indicate common grammar, punctuation, sentence boundary, and academic word choice issues. Match each highlighted section with its mention in the box at the bottom of the essay.

Annotations

A. A form of punctuation should appear after this item in the source listing. Add the missing punctuation mark.

B. This passage needs to punctuation to introduce the quotation. Add the missing punctuation.

C. This sentence needs a comma after an introductory word or phrase. Add the comma in the correct place.

D. These sentences are fragments. Rewrite them to fix the error.

E. This passage has multiple run-on sentences. Rewrite the passage without run-on sentences.

F. This sentence uses the second-person (the word "your") in a confusing way. Rewrite the sentence to avoid the word "your."

G. This sentence has an extra period. Remove the unneeded one. This sentence lacks parallelism. Change the sentence to make all parts parallel.

H. These citations are not listed correctly. Place them in the correct order.

I. This passage announces the author's goal in an awkward way. Rewrite the passage to avoid the announcement.

Figure A.4a. Student Essay Sample. Page 1.

Answer: _____

Explanation: _____

_____

_____

_____

_____

_____

_____

_____

Nice work! This word can be easy to confuse with "its," so well done using the apostrophe.

Name   1

Student Name

Instructor Name

Course Name

Due Date

"Warning! Challenges ahead!" would be a great motto for individuals who embark on the journey of juggling work, life, school, and obligations while in college. A majority of college students who work and attend school. Find balance to be a real struggle. Life is often challenging; balancing work and school while also attempting to meet other demands that scream for attention can easily become overwhelming. There can be many obstacles to navigate in all aspects of life, and college is not an exception. Students who work while attending college have increased stress because it's an additional layer of responsibility. It's important that students manage their time well and have good strong support systems to help them navigate barriers or potential barriers that can hinder progress or threaten their goals.

Managing multiple responsibilities is a real stressor that can lead to burn out, otherwise known as exhaustion from overwork. Students should prioritize self care and incorporate healthy boundaries and habits to reduce stress. "For some students, working full-time may even be a necessity which

Figure A.4b. Student Essay Sample. Page 2.

Name   2

can lead to a neglect of self care."(Estrada 2). Estrada speaks with former

academic advisor Jennifer Wonderly, who discusses the signs of

overworking: "Missing class is a huge one, and sometimes they're missing

class due to work or just from oversleeping because they are physically

exhausted" said Wonderly "My experience in academic advising is that when

students go on academic probation, it's usually not because of not having the

academic ability, it's usually due to time management issues and competing

obligations" (qtd. In Estrada). When work is absolutely essential to meeting

basic needs, this ranks the priority, and automatically appoints work as a

greater importance and school by default is secondary to that. Megan Sovona,

a current college student working full time claims, "Time becomes even more

valuable when balancing work, life and school. Sadly I don't have the option

to work less, if anything I find myself needing to work more just to cover all

the bills. Finding extra time to relax and unwind is challenging. Something

always needs to get done and the never ending "to do" list can be

exhausting." Sovona stresses the significance of having good communication

and support from her college academic advisors and to be aware of the

programs colleges offer. "Take advantage of the programs offered, they can

be a huge asset in helping you achieve your goals and overcome obstacles.

Answer: _____

Explanation:_____

_____

_____

_____

_____

_____

Answer: _____

Explanation:_____

_____

_____

_____

_____

_____

Answer: _____

Explanation:_____

_____

_____

_____

_____

_____

Figure A.4c. Student Essay Sample. Page 3.

Answer: _____

Explanation: _____

_____

_____

_____

_____

_____

_____

_____

Answer: _____

Explanation: _____

_____

_____

_____

_____

_____

_____

_____

Name   3

Don't be afraid to ask for help," says Sovona. Time is a finite resource for working students. Understanding the negative impact work and school related stress impose on students they should make time in their hectic schedules for self care and make use of helpful resources.

Pursuing a degree that is in second place on the priority list is a significant challenge in itself. I try to give each responsibility equal priority, but I work full time while pursuing a degree. Working full time is non negotiable. I have a mortgage, I have family, I have commitments and obligations. Balancing all of this is stressful, especially when work conflicts with school obligations. As a mandatory worker within a hospital, I recently had to stay over four hours on my scheduled shift, unfortunately it was on a day when two writing quizzes were due. I arrived home with less than 30 minutes to brush up on material and take the quizzes, sadly I did not do as well as I could have. When incidents like this happen, I have no choice but to choose work. My experience has also shown me that proper planning and time management, as well as keeping your employer well informed and expressing your needs, can lessen the impact work will have on school life. For me, time management plays a remarkable role in how things balance out. Everything must be scheduled and prioritized. I have to be purposeful in how

Figure A.4d. Student Essay Sample. Page 4.

Name   4

I spend my time. If I have scheduled a block of time to work on a paper, I have to be unwilling to surrender that priority in order to watch a movie with my family.

In this essay, I want to talk about how, when I start to feel overwhelmed and pulled in too many directions, I stop and prioritize my health. I have a constant list of things that need to be accomplished and that list gets prioritized as well. These little tasks don't sound like much, but compounded on top of all the other obligations and responsibilities, it makes the balancing act more difficult and time consuming. It's important to trust in my own ability and believe I have what it takes to successfully manage and balance work, school, and life demands. I suggest to anyone who is working while attending school, to keep your family posted and up to date on what's going on. My family's support and encouragement is a tremendous help. It allows me the capacity to focus on school, making it a commensurate priority to work.

Does working while attending college increase stress due to additional responsibility? According to Mental Health America's website, "Feeling overloaded can seriously damage your mind and body, making you more vulnerable to physical and mental health problems. Additionally, chronic

Becoming a College Writer: *A Student Workbook*

Figure A.4e. Student Essay Sample. Page 5.

Name   5

stress keeps you from being your best self. While stress is not inherently bad, it's important to find healthy ways to deal with it." ("Balancing Work and School"). For many students, working is a necessity while attending college. It is a struggle that adds stressors in their lives. Time becomes such a valuable commodity that self neglect often occurs. To avoid fewer bumps in the road, it is crucial to make self care a priority to avoid burnout. Something I do to help avoid burnout is to make sure I have one day a week that is completely free from work and school responsibilities. I do have to plan properly and make sure the majority of course and study work is completed to achieve this.

When students are struggling to make ends meet, it is important that they educate themselves and utilize the programs available through school and within the community and asking for help when needed. College students should manage their time well, prioritizing and scheduling intelligently, and to stick to those commitments. Working students should also communicate and express their needs to employers in this way students maximize their potential success of balancing school and work.

Excellent! The singular verb "is" correctly matches the singular noun "majority."

Answer: _____

Explanation: _____

_____

_____

_____

_____

_____

_____

_____

122

Figure A.4f. Student Essay Sample. Page 6.

Name   6

Works Cited

Sovona, Megan. Interview with author. 20 Oct. 2021.

Estrada, Reyna. "How to Maintain a Healthy Work Life Balance in College."

University Wire, Apr. 25, 2019. *ProQuest*, www-proquest-

com.chemeketa.idm.oclc.org/docview/2214416114.

"Balancing Work and School." *Mental Health America*,

www.mhanational.org/balancing-work-and-school. Accessed 31 Oct.

2021.

Answer: _____

Explanation: _____

_____

_____

_____

_____

_____

_____

_____

_____

Glossary

apostrophe: (') A punctuation mark that
1) replaces missing letters in contractions,
2) indicates possession, or
3) makes a single-letter word plural.
65–71, 118

attribution: A way of introducing an idea that comes from another source. This might be an attributive phrase, such as "According to …".
56, 79

brainstorming: An individual or group problem-solving activity that involves generating multiple ideas without judgment. This is a common prewriting exercise.
2–4

capitalization: The use of an upper case letter to show the beginning of a sentence or to differentiate between proper nouns and common nouns.
79–83

citation: A way of showing where an idea comes from. This includes in-text citations and end-of-paper citations.
24, 40

comma: (,) A punctuation mark that is used to divide ideas from one another. This happens with lists of items, multiple clauses, introductory ideas, interruptions to main ideas, introductions to quotations and attributions, multi-part numbers and nouns, and sometimes just to avoid confusion.
50–52, 72–78, 108

comma splice: A writing error caused by two independent clauses joined with a comma. This creates a run-on sentence.
51, 53

conclusion: A closing paragraph or paragraphs in a paper that 1) shows how the body paragraphs have explained and defended the thesis of the paper and 2) looks to the future implications of that thesis being true.
14, 31–32

contraction: Two words combined into one with an apostrophe standing in for the missing letter(s).
65–69

conventions: A set of expectations; in academic writing, this includes using correct grammar, punctuation, spelling, formatting, and citations.
19, 22

coordinating conjunction: One of seven specific conjunctions—and, but, or, yet, for, nor, so—that join parts of a sentence.
50–53, 73, 88

drafting: The act of writing that involves developing your thesis with supporting ideas. This part of the writing process follows planning and prewriting.
17–18

editing: The act of making changes to word choice, sentences, or organization in a piece of writing to improve its overall quality. This is often one of the final steps of the writing process.
22–25

FANBOYS: (see coordinating conjunction)

fragment: An incomplete sentence.
42–47

freewriting: An idea-generating activity that involves writing as quickly as possible without stopping to make corrections. This is a common prewriting activity.
6–11, 17

gerund: A noun formed from a verb by adding "–ing" to the end.
89

infinitive: A noun or adverb phrase formed by "to" plus the root form of a verb and indicating no specific tense.
89

introduction: An opening paragraph that introduces three pieces of information that will appear in your paper: 1) the topic of your paper, 2) the focus of your paper on a part of that topic, and 3) the main idea (thesis) that your paper will explain.
14, 31–32, 36

www.ingramcontent.com/pod-product-compliance
Lightning Source LLC
Chambersburg PA
CBHW080608090426
42735CB00017B/3361